Weather and Climate Inventory National Park Service Central Alaska Network

Natural Resource Technical Report NPS/CAKN/NRTR—2006/004

WRCC Report WRCC 06-01

Kelly T. Redmond and David B. Simeral
Western Regional Climate Center
Desert Research Institute
2215 Raggio Parkway
Reno, Nevada 89512-1095

August 2006

U.S. Department of the Interior
National Park Service
Natural Resource Program Center
Fort Collins, Colorado

The Natural Resource Publication series addresses natural resource topics that are of interest and applicability to a broad readership in the National Park Service and to others in the management of natural resources, including the scientific community, the public, and the National Park Service conservation and environmental constituencies. Manuscripts are peer-reviewed to ensure that the information is scientifically credible, technically accurate, appropriately written for the intended audience, and designed and published in a professional manner.

The Natural Resource Technical Reports series is used to disseminate the peer-reviewed results of scientific studies in the physical, biological, and social sciences for both the advancement of science and the achievement of the National Park Service's mission. The reports provide contributors with a forum for displaying comprehensive data that are often deleted from journals because of page limitations. Current examples of such reports include the results of research that addresses natural resource management issues; natural resource inventory and monitoring activities; resource assessment reports; scientific literature reviews; and peer reviewed proceedings of technical workshops, conferences, or symposia.

Printed copies of reports in these series may be produced in a limited quantity and they are only available as long as the supply lasts. This report is also available from the Natural Resource Publications Management website (http://www.nature.nps.gov/publications/NRPM) on the Internet or by sending a request to the address on the back cover.

Please cite this publication as follows:

Redmond, K. T., and D. B. Simeral. 2006. Weather and Climate Inventory, National Park Service, Central Alaska Network. Natural Resource Technical Report NPS/CAKN/NRTR—2006/004. National Park Service, Fort Collins, Colorado.

NPS/CAKN/NRTR—2006/004, August 2006

Contents

CONTENTS (continued)

Figures

Tables

Appendixes

Acronyms

AASC	American Association of State Climatologists
ACIS	Applied Climate Information System
AIRMoN	Atmospheric Integrated Research Monitoring Network
ASOS	Automated Surface Observing System
AWOS	Automated Weather Observing System
BIA	Bureau of Indian Affairs
BLM	Bureau of Land Management
CAKN	Central Alaska I&M Network
CASTNet	Clean Air Status and Trends Network
C-MAN	Coastal Marine Automated Network
COOP	Cooperative Observer Program
CRN	Climate Reference Network
DENA	Denali National Park and Preserve
DFIR	Double-Fence Intercomparison Reference
DRI	Desert Research Institute
DST	Daylight Savings Time
ENSO	El Niño / Southern Oscillation
EPA	Environmental Protection Agency
FAA	Federal Aviation Administration
FIPS	Federal Information Processing Standards
FWS	Fish and Wildlife Service
GMT	Greenwich Mean Time
GOES	Geostationary Operational Environmental Satellite
GPMP	NPS Gaseous Pollutant Monitoring Program
GPS	Global Positioning System
HCN	Historical Climatology Network
I&M	NPS Inventory and Monitoring Program
LAMPS	Lighthouse Automation and Modernization Program
LST	Local Standard Time
LTEM	NPS Long Term Environmental Monitoring
MDN	Mercury Deposition Network
NADP	National Atmospheric Deposition Program
NCDC	National Climatic Data Center
NCEP	National Centers for Environmental Prediction
NDBC	National Data Buoy Center
NIFC	National Interagency Fire Center
NOAA	National Oceanic and Atmospheric Administration
NPS	National Park Service
NRCS	Natural Resources Conservation Service
NRCS-AM	USDA / NRCS Aerial Marker
NRCS-SC	USDA / NRCS Snow Course
NTN	National Trends Network
NWS	National Weather Service
PDO	Pacific Decadal Oscillation

PRISM	Parameter Regression on Independent Slopes Model
RAWS	Remote Automated Weather Station Network
RCC	Regional Climate Center
SAO	Surface Airways Observations Program
SC	USDA / NRCS snowcourse
Surfrad	Surface Radiation Budget Network
SNOTEL	Snowfall Telemetry Network
SOD	Summary-of-the-Day
SWAN	NPS Southwest Alaska I&M Network
USDA	U.S. Department of Agriculture
USFS	United States Forest Service
USGS	U.S. Geological Survey
UTC	Coordinated Universal Time
WMO	World Meteorological Organization
WRCC	Western Regional Climate Center
WRST	Wrangell-St. Elias National Park and Preserve
YUCH	Yukon-Charley Rivers National Preserve

Executive Summary

Climate is a dominant factor driving the physical and ecologic processes affecting the Central Alaska Inventory and Monitoring Network (CAKN). Climate behavior also has numerous practical and management consequences and implications. Extreme weather and climate phenomena are near or beyond survival limits for many forms of life. Evidence and projections in the CAKN region point to potentially significant long-term climate change, affecting temperature and type of precipitation. These would have importance consequences for ice masses, permafrost, vegetation, chemical exchanges between the atmosphere and soil, and microbial, floral and faunal biology.

This project was initiated to inventory past and present climate monitoring efforts. In this report, we provide the following information:

- Overview of broad-scale climatic factors and zones important to CAKN park units.
- Inventory of weather and climate station locations in and near CAKN park units relevant to the NPS I&M Program.
- Results of an inventory of metadata on each weather station, including affiliations for weather-monitoring networks, types of measurements recorded at these stations, and information about the actual measurements (length of record, etc.).
- Initial evaluation of the adequacy of coverage for existing weather stations and recommendations for improvements in monitoring weather and climate.

Two park units (Denali National Park and Preserve – DENA; Wrangell-St. Elias National Park and Preserve – WRST) span the transition from maritime influence to interior influence, while the remaining unit (Yukon-Charley Rivers National Preserve - YUCH) is more nearly characterized by a single general (interior) influence. Temporal variability is of great significance for CAKN, especially two modes. One encompasses variability on the half-century time scale (Pacific Decadal Variability) reflecting ocean behavior to the south, and the other is related to recent high latitude manifestations of climate change.

Through a search of national databases and inquiries to NPS staff, we have identified 114 weather and climate stations in or near CAKN park units. These include 40 stations for DENA, 58 stations for WRST, and 16 stations for YUCH. Phase 1, 2, and 3 vital signs monitoring plans, draft protocols, numerous prospective standard operating procedures, field reconnaissance visit descriptions, and other background material were consulted and proved very beneficial. Climate records and metadata accessible to the Western Regional Climate Center (WRCC) were consulted to help judge actual performance of existing and developing measurement programs.

This report has benefited greatly from excellent work by the CAKN network staff, who have done a thorough job in developing and following a methodology for evaluation of their climate monitoring activities. They have enlisted outside cooperators as needed and have incorporated such input into their planning process. Their plans, strategies and ongoing implementation appear to be well thought out. The CAKN staff have helped advance philosophical underpinnings for the National Park Service Inventory and Monitoring (NPS I&M) program as a whole and for weather and climate in particular. At the same time, the CAKN staff have retained the practical focus that is much needed in this harsh environment.

The main goal of climate monitoring is tracking through time. Station densities for this purpose are low in these vast tracts, which are among the largest in the national park system. Existing and planned stations appear suitably distributed to capture the largest spatially coherent regional patterns in trend and variability. Strategies for addressing the significant spatial differences in climate by utilizing transects across gradients, or small-scale dense clustering, are well-founded.

Given the large areas, long-term measurements from within the boundaries are quite scarce, with none to at most a few per park unit. The record from DENA at McKinley Park is the longest, covering 8 decades. Such key long term measurements merit high priority for continued operation into the indefinite future, preferably with no changes in methods or sites. Records from WRST are broken into segments from different locations. Multi-decade records do not exist within YUCH; the longest continuous station has a mere 16-year record, and these do not include all-weather precipitation. Thus, external records from the National Oceanic and Atmospheric Administration will remain as the principal proxy source of data for YUCH for many years, and leveraging activities to help insure their continuation should be under way.

Logistics and a demanding climate pose special challenges. Winters are punishing on instruments, batteries, and solar chargers, and special precautions and backup procedures are strongly recommended. In snowy, harsh and alpine environments credible observations are going to be more expensive and difficult than in other more benign settings, often costing initially and annually 2-3 times what a conveniently accessible back yard station might.

Stations in these environments likely have to survive on their own for extended periods without maintenance or inspection. Components and configurations that are "battle-tested" in similar environments should be utilized. Skilled and experienced technicians are a necessity, and methods to develop and retain such valued people should be present. In the end, rich prior experience has shown that maintenance always proves to be the most important ingredient in a successful monitoring program.

Acknowledgements

This work was supported and completed under Task Agreement H8R07010001, with the Great Basin Cooperative Ecosystem Studies Unit. We would like to acknowledge very helpful assistance from various National Park Service personnel in southern and central Alaska. Particular thanks for excellent comments (and patience) are extended to Pam Sousanes, John Gross, Steve Garman, and Margaret Beer of NPS, and to Christopher Davey, Grant Kelly, Greg McCurdy and Heather Angeloff of WRCC. Portions of the work were also supported by the WRCC.

1.0 Introduction

Weather and climate are key drivers in ecosystem structure and function. Global- and regional-scale climate variations have a tremendous impact on natural systems (Chapin, et al., 1996; Schlesinger 1997; Jacobson et al. 2000; Bonan 2002; Redmond, 2006). Long-term patterns in temperature and precipitation provide first-order constraints on potential ecosystem structure and function. Secondary constraints are realized from the intensity and duration of individual weather events and, additionally, from seasonality and inter-annual climate variability. These constraints influence the fundamental properties of ecologic systems, such as soil–water relationships, plant–soil processes, and nutrient cycling, as well as disturbance rates and intensity. These properties, in turn, influence the life-history strategies supported by a climatic regime (Neilson 1987).

Climate behavior also has numerous practical and management consequences and implications. Extreme weather and climate phenomena are near or beyond survival limits for many forms of life. Evidence and projections in the CAKN region point to potentially significant long-term climate change, affecting temperature and type of precipitation. These would have importance consequences for ice masses, permafrost, vegetation, chemical exchanges between the atmosphere and soil, and microbial, floral and faunal biology.

The purpose of this report is to determine the current status of weather and climate monitoring in the Central Alaska Network (CAKN) of the National Park Service (NPS) Inventory and Monitoring (I&M) Program. The three units that comprise CAKN are Denali National Park and Preserve (DENA), Wrangell-St. Elias National Park and Preserve (WRST), and Yukon-Charley Rivers National Preserve (YUCH) (Figure 1.1). These park units have been organized into the CAKN for the purposes of carrying out ecological monitoring activities under the NPS I&M program. The broad goals of the CAKN monitoring program are to: (1) better understand the dynamic nature and condition of park ecosystems; and (2) provide reference points for comparisons with other, altered environments (MacCluskie et al. 2004). The focus of the CAKN program will be to monitor ecosystems in order to detect change in ecological components and in the relationships among the components.

The CAKN draft climate protocols (Sousanes and Adema 2004) further specify the climate monitoring objectives for this I&M network:

- Record long-term trends in temperature and precipitation through fully instrumented sites placed in the parks at representative areas, and maintain the integrity of existing National Weather Service (NWS) Cooperative sites with long-term records.
- Record long-term trends in secondary climate drivers such as wind speed, solar radiation, and relative humidity. These measurements provide information on the localized climate. These data are also very useful indicators for fire ecology.
- Distribute data in convenient formats to evaluate the influence of local and global climate cycles on resources within the ecosystem.

The CAKN Climate Monitoring program objectives will greatly enhance our knowledge of the changing climate system and provide a robust baseline to assess changes directly related to changes in the physical environment.

In this report, we provide the following informational elements:

- Overview of broad-scale climatic factors and zones important to CAKN park units.
- Inventory of locations for all weather stations in and near CAKN park units that are relevant to the NPS I&M networks.
- Results of metadata inventory for each station, including weather-monitoring network affiliations, types of recorded measurements, and information about actual measurements (length of record, etc.).
- Initial evaluation of the adequacy of coverage for existing weather stations and recommendations for improvements in monitoring weather and climate.

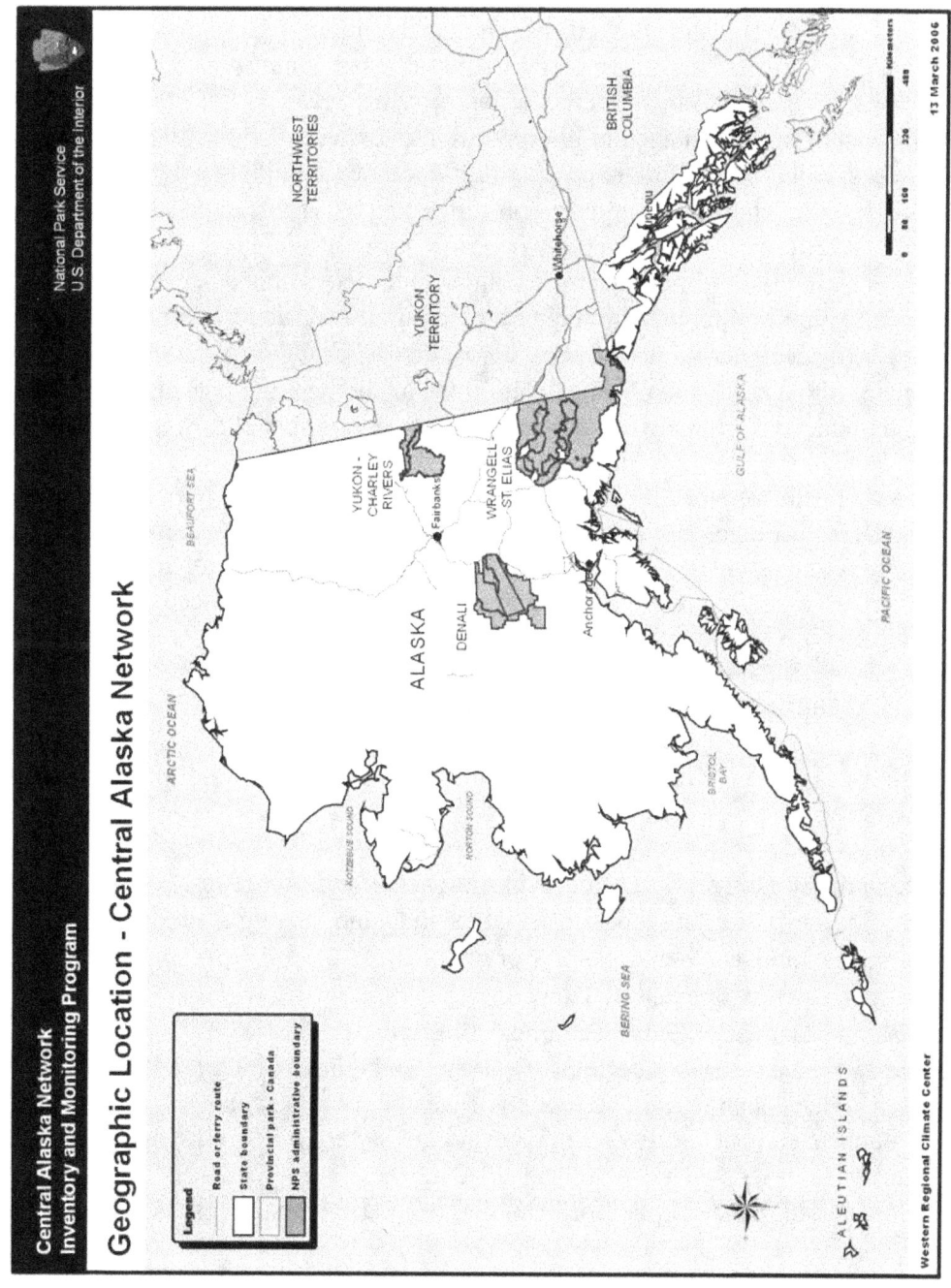

Figure 1.1. Map of the Central Alaska Inventory and Monitoring Network (CAKN).

3

1.1 Purpose of Measurements

Weather and climate data and information constitute a prominent and widely requested component of the NPS I&M networks (I&M 2006). As primary environmental drivers for the other "vital signs," weather and climate patterns present various practical and management consequences and implications for the NPS (Oakley et al. 2003). Within the context of the NPS, the following services constitute the main purposes for recording weather and climate observations:

- Provide measurements for real-time operational needs and early warnings of potential hazards (landslides, mudflows, washouts, fallen trees, plowing activities, fire conditions, aircraft and watercraft conditions, road conditions, rescue conditions, fog, restoration and remediation activities, etc.).
- Provide visitor education and aid interpretation of expected and actual conditions for visitors while they are in the park and for deciding if and when to visit the park.
- Establish engineering and design criteria for structures, roads, culverts, etc., for human comfort, safety, and economic needs.
- Consistently monitor climate over the long-term to detect changes in environmental drivers affecting ecosystems, including both gradual and sudden events.
- Provide retrospective data to understand *a posteriori* changes in flora and fauna.
- Document for posterity the physical conditions in and near the park units, including mean, extreme, and variable measurements (in time and space) for all applications.

The last three items in the preceding list are pertinent primarily to the NPS I&M networks; however, all items are important to NPS operations and management. Most of the needs in this list overlap heavily. It is often impractical to operate separate climate measuring systems that also cannot be used to meet ordinary weather needs, where there is greater emphasis on timeliness and reliability.

1.2 Design of Climate Monitoring Programs

The evaluation and design of either an optimal or sufficient climate monitoring program that serves NPS needs includes these processes:

- Define park and network-specific monitoring needs and objectives.
- Identify locations and data repositories of existing and historic stations.
- Acquire existing data when necessary or practical.
- Evaluate the quality of existing data.
- Evaluate the adequacy of coverage of existing stations.
- Develop a protocol for monitoring the weather and climate, including the following:
  o Standardized summaries and reports of weather/climate data.
  o Data management (quality assurance and quality control, archiving, data access, etc.).
- Develop and implement a plan for installing or modifying stations, as necessary.

Throughout the design process, there are various factors that require consideration in evaluating weather and climate measurements. Many of these factors have been summarized by Dr. Tom Karl, director of the NOAA National Climatic Data Center (NCDC), and widely distributed as the "Ten Principles for Climate Monitoring" (Karl et al. 1996; National Research Council, 2001). These principles are presented in Appendix A, and the guidelines are embodied in many of the comments made throughout this report. The most critical factors are presented here. In addition, an overview of requirements necessary to operate a climate network is provided in Appendix C, with further discussion in Appendix E.

1.2.1 Need for Consistency

A principal goal in climate monitoring is to detect and characterize slow and sudden changes in climate through time. This is of less concern for day-to-day weather changes, but it is of paramount importance for climate change. There are many ways whereby changes in techniques for making measurements, changes in instruments or their exposures, or seemingly innocuous changes in site characteristics can lead to apparent changes in climate. Safeguards must be in place to avoid these false sources of temporal "climate" variability if we are to draw correct inferences about real climate behavior over time from archived measurements.

For climate monitoring, consistency through time is vital, counting at least as importantly as absolute accuracy. Sensors record only what is occurring at the sensor—this is all they can really "know." It is the responsibility of station or station network managers to ensure that observations are representative of the spatial and temporal climate scales that we wish to record.

1.2.2 Metadata

Changes in sensors, site conditions, and observing methods can cause produce artificial changes in the climate record. It is therefore necessary to document all factors that can bear on the interpretation of climate measurements and to update the information repeatedly through time. This information ("metadata," data about data) has its own history and set of quality-control issues that parallel those of the actual measured data. There is no single standard for the content of climate metadata, but a simple rule suffices:

- Observers should record all information that could be needed in the future to interpret observations correctly, long after they are available to assist.

Such documentation includes notes, drawings, site forms, and photos, which can be of inestimable value if taken in the correct manner. That stated, it is not always clear to the metadata provider *what is important* for posterity and *what will be important* in the future. It is almost impossible to "over document" a station. Station documentation is underappreciated greatly and seldom thorough enough (especially for climate purposes). Insufficient attention to this issue often lowers the present and especially future value of otherwise useful data.

5

The convention followed throughout climatology is to refer to metadata as information about the measurement process, station circumstances, and data. The term "data" is reserved solely for the actual weather and climate records obtained from sensors.

1.2.3 Maintenance

Inattention to maintenance is the greatest source of failure in weather/climate stations and networks. Problems can begin to occur soon after sites are deployed. A regular visit schedule must be implemented, where sites, settings (e.g., vegetation), sensors, communications, and data flow are checked routinely (once or twice a year at a minimum) and updated as necessary. Most parts must be changed out for recalibration (annual) or replacement. With adequate maintenance, at automated sites the entire instrument suite should be replaced or completely refurbished about once every five to seven years.

Simple preventative maintenance is effective but requires much planning and skilled technical staff. Changes in technology and products require retraining and continual re-education. Travel, logistics, scheduling, and seasonal access restrictions consume major amounts of time and budget but are absolutely necessary. Without such attention, data gradually become less credible and then often are misused or not used at all.

1.2.4 Automated versus Manual Stations

Historic stations often have depended on manual observations and many continue to operate in this mode. Manual observations frequently produce excellent data sets. Sensors and data are simple and intuitive, well tested, and relatively cheap. Manual stations have much to offer in certain circumstances and can be a source of both primary and backup data. However, methodical consistency for manual measurements is a constant challenge, especially with a mobile work force. Operating manual stations takes time and affects schedules, though sometimes the imposed routine is regarded as welcome.

Nearly all newer stations are automated. Automated stations provide better time resolution, increased (though imperfect) reliability, greater capacity for data storage, and improved accessibility to large amounts of data. The purchase cost for automated stations is higher than for manual stations. A common expectation and serious misconception is that an automated station can be deployed and left to operate on its own. In reality, automation does not eliminate the need for people but rather changes the type of person that is needed. Skilled technical personnel are needed and must be readily available, especially if live communications exist and data gaps are not wanted. Site visits are needed at least annually and spare parts must be maintained. Typical annual costs for sensors and maintenance are $1.5–2.5K per station per year.

1.2.5 Communications

With manual stations, the observer is responsible for recording and transmitting station data. Data from automated stations, however, can be transmitted quickly for access by research and operations personnel, which is a highly preferable situation. A comparison of communication systems for automated and manual stations shows that automated stations generally require additional equipment, more power, higher-transmission costs, attention to sources of disruption or garbling, and backup procedures (such as manual downloads from data loggers).

Automated stations are capable of functioning normally without communication and can retain many months of data. At such sites, however, alerts about station problems are not possible, large gaps can accrue when accessible stations quit, and the constituencies needed to support such stations are smaller and less vocal. Two-way communications permit full recovery from disruptions, ability to reprogram data loggers remotely, and better opportunities for diagnostics and troubleshooting. In virtually all cases, two-way communications are much preferred to all other communication methods. However, two-way communications require considerations of cost, signal access, transmission rates, interference, and methods for keeping sensor and communication power loops separate. Two-way communications are frequently impossible (no service) or impractical, expensive, or power consumptive. Two-way methods (cellular, land line, radio, internet) require smaller up-front costs as compared to other methods of communication and have variable recurrent costs, starting at zero. Satellite links work everywhere (except when blocked by trees or cliffs) and are quite reliable but are one-way and relatively slow, allow no re-transmissions, and require high up-front costs ($3–4K) but have no recurrent costs. Communications technology is changing constantly and requires vigilant attention by maintenance personnel to react to business decisions in a competitive industry.

1.2.6 Quality Assurance and Quality Control

Quality control and quality assurance are issues at every step through the entire sequence of sensing, communication, storage, retrieval, and display of environmental data. Quality assurance is an umbrella concept that covers all data collection and processing (start-to-finish) and ensures that credible information is available to the end user. Quality control has a more limited scope and is defined by the International Standards Organization as "the operational techniques and activities that are used to satisfy quality requirements." The central problem can be better appreciated if we think of quality control in the following manner.

- Quality control is the evaluation, assessment, and rehabilitation of imperfect data by making use of other imperfect data.

Once an observation is made, its quality can only decrease with time. The best and most effective quality control, therefore, consists in making high-quality measurements from the start and then successfully transmitting the measurements to an ingest process and storage site. Once the data are received from a monitoring station, a series of checks with increasing complexity can be applied, ranging from single-element checks (self-consistency) to multiple-element checks (inter-sensor consistency) to multiple-station/single-element checks (inter-station consistency). Suitable ancillary data (battery voltages, data ranges for all measurements, etc.) can prove extremely useful in diagnosing problems.

With measurements, there is rarely a single technique that will work satisfactorily for all situations. Quality-control procedures must be tailored to individual station circumstances, data access and storage methods, and climate regimes.

The fundamental issue in quality control centers on the tradeoff between falsely rejecting good data (Type I error) and falsely accepting bad data (Type II error). We cannot reduce the incidence of one type of error without increasing the incidence of the other type. In weather and climate data assessments, Type I errors are deemed far less desirable than Type II errors.

Not all observations are equal. Quality-control procedures are likely to have the most difficulty with the most important (extreme) observations, where independent information usually must be sought and incorporated. Quality control at the reliability level desired by most users usually involves a great deal of infrastructure that has its own (imperfect) error-detection methods, which must be in place before a single value can be evaluated.

1.2.7 Standards

Although there is near-universal recognition of the value in systematic weather and climate measurements, these measurements will have little value unless they conform to accepted standards. There is not a single source for standards for collecting weather and climate data nor a single standard that meets all needs. Measurement standards have been developed by the American Association of State Climatologists (AASC 1985, primarily for agricultural applications), U.S. Environmental Protection Agency (EPA 1987), World Meteorological Organization (WMO 1983; 2005), Finklin and Fischer (1990), National Wildfire Coordinating Group (2004), and RAWS program (Bureau of Land Management [BLM] 1997). Variations to these measurement standards also have been offered by instrument makers (e.g., Tanner 1990).

1.2.8 Visibility, Aesthetics, and Interpretation

This issue arises frequently enough to deserve comment. Standards for quality climate measurements require open exposures away from heat sources, buildings, pavement, close vegetation and tall trees, and human intrusion (thus away from property lines). By their nature, sites that meet these standards are usually quite visible. In many settings (such as heavily forested areas) these sites also are quite rare, making them precisely the same places that managers wish to protect from aesthetic intrusion. For these reasons, the most suitable and scientifically defensible sites frequently are rejected as candidate locations for weather/climate stations. Most weather/climate stations, therefore, tend to be "hidden" but many of these hidden locations have inferior exposures. Some measure of compromise is nearly always called for in siting weather and climate stations.

1.3 Weather versus Climate Definitions

It is important to distinguish whether the primary use of a given station is for weather purposes or for climate purposes.

- "Weather" generally refers to instantaneous conditions in the atmosphere.
- "Climate" refers to the complete and entire ensemble of statistical descriptors of the temporal and spatial properties of the behavior of the atmosphere.

The question of whether climate acts as the enabler of weather, or weather summarizes to constitute climate, will not be resolved here. Our understanding of climate has changed markedly in the past quarter century, with a far greater appreciation that climate is dynamic, as much about change as about stasis. Climate and weather phenomena shade gradually into each other, and are ultimately inseparable.

Weather station networks are intended for near-real-time usage, where the precise circumstances of a set of measurements are typically less important. In these cases, changes in exposure or other attributes over time are not as critical. Climate networks, however, are intended for long-term tracking of atmospheric conditions. Siting and exposure are critical factors for climate networks, and it is vitally important that the observational circumstances remain essentially unchanged over the duration of the station record. Some climate networks can be considered hybrids of weather/climate networks, wherein data meeting climate standards are rapidly supplied to serve purposes on the short-term "weather" time scale.

2.0 Climate Background

This section provides general climate background and introduces some of the major CAKN climate issues and concerns for the I&M program which are further discussed in Section 5. Sousanes and Adema (2004) provided a comprehensive summary that goes into detail about a number of aspects of CAKN climate, and especially those that relate to measurement and associated logistics.

A special and major feature of the CAKN is the presence of numerous active glaciers and glacial phenomena. These both affect and are affected by climate, and can also serve as climatic indicators. As noted by CAKN (2004), this region contains the largest assemblage of glaciers and greatest collection of peaks over 5,000 meters in elevation in the NPS. The Nabesna Glacier is the world's longest interior valley glacier (over 120 km long), the Malaspina Glacier is North America's largest piedmont glacier (nearly 70 km across), the Hubbard Glacier##### is the longest tidewater glacier in Alaska (over 120 km long with an open calving face covering over 10 km), and the Bagley Icefield is the largest subpolar icefield in North America. Glaciers in Alaska have retreated over the past century and continue to do so (BESIS 1997). The USGS Glacier and Snow Program is tracking a number of glaciers in Alaska (<ak.water.usgs.gov/glaciology/Default.htm>) and in some places has monitoring instruments.

2.1 Spatial Variability

The three park units of CAKN span an area extending 650 km in north-south and east-west directions, at latitudes from 60 to 65 N. Elevations range from sea level to 6194 m. These units contain 12 of the 32 unified ecoregions of Alaska and include the highest mountains and some of the larger rivers in North America. Climate in this vast area exhibits extreme spatial variability, ranging from strongly maritime to strongly continental, with large differences in temperature and precipitation.

The spatial patterns of the annual cycle of mean monthly precipitation and temperature are illustrated by four locations in Figure 2.1. Cordova is on the coast just west of the Copper River delta; Tonsina is 100 km northeast of Cordova along the Copper River on the west side of WRST; Eagle is on the Yukon River just inside the US-Canada border in far eastern YUCH; McKinley Park is at the entrance to the DENA access road. Along much of the coast (Cordova), the dry season is in spring and the wet season is in late summer and autumn. Just a short distance inland the transition to a more uniform seasonal precipitation distribution becomes evident at Tonsina. The further transition toward a summer-centered precipitation regime is seen at Eagle and McKinley Park stations. Storms usually do not penetrate far inland from winter into spring, so in the interior this is usually the dry season, and the high sun months are the wettest. We have chosen March and September to represent the climatologically driest and wettest times of the year for the CAKN region; this approximation is more nearly correct along the coast than inland.

2.1.1 Precipitation

The southern portion of CAKN is a region where Pacific storms often decay and die, and is frequently is influenced by cool, moist systems that follow a trajectory around the southern end of the Aleutian Low. This area is by far the wettest within these three park units. Indeed, the southeast portion of WRST has locations that are viable candidates for the wettest location in the world (Chris Daly, personal communication), where PRISM (Parameter Regression on Independent Slopes Method; Daly et al. 1994; Daly et al. 2002; Gibson et al. 2002; Doggett et al. 2004) estimates of annual precipitation reach as high as 12000 mm (Figure 2.2), among the wettest spots on Earth. The icefields in southern WRST receive 3000-7000 mm of precipitation annually, and above about 1500 m most of this precipitation falls as snow. The transition to drier climates is occurs over a very short distance. Along the Chitina River on the north side of the SE coastal ice fields, the annual precipitation is as low as 300-500 mm. The central mountain peaks of WRST (Mt. Sanford, Mt. Wrangell, etc.) receive "only" 2000-3000 mm of precipitation. On the north side of the Mt. Sanford – Mt. Wrangell complex, annual precipitation declines to only 200-300 mm.

Contrasting precipitation in March to that in September for the CAKN portion of the state (Figure 2.3 and Figure 2.4), in both months the coastal strip is much wetter than elsewhere. March is especially dry inland compared with September; the gradient of relative precipitation (normalized to the coast) is less in late summer, when nearly every location is somewhat wet, than it is in spring.

Through their own presence the mountains augment the precipitation experienced in their vicinity, with the result that within overall climate regimes, precipitation patterns often look very similar to those of the major topographic elements.

2.1.2 Temperature

Mean annual temperature for the CAKN area is shown in Figure 2.5, and mean monthly maximum and minimum temperatures in the extreme coldest months (Figures 2.6-2.7) and warmest months (Figure 2.8-2.9), to encompass the range of typical extremes. All of these have physical and ecological significance. They show that the interior is (much) colder than the coast in winter, but warmer than the coast in summer. With the high sun in summer, there is relatively little spatial variation in minimum temperature from the coast to the interior in summer, except for the effects arising from elevation. All of these characteristics are readily explainable on physical grounds.

Figure 2.5 is deliberately shaded to emphasize the fact that the CAKN area near the coast experiences an annual average temperature that is close to freezing. This has important implications for those locations that are heavily glaciated. Given the sensitive dependence of glaciers on temperature, much of the ice in this area seems vulnerable to even slight warming (assuming no major changes in precipitation amount or seasonality). In many places only a small shift in temperatures will change the climatic regime from one where temperatures are largely near freezing and slightly below freezing to one where temperatures are near freezing to slightly above freezing. All the areas in yellow on Figure 2.5 experience average annual temperatures between 0 and -2°C, and a modest climate warming of +2°C would increase the areal coverage and the fraction of the year with above-freezing temperatures, with potentially significant consequences. It is readily apparent that there are large areas in this circumstance. Some of the ice in this part of the state is flowing downward from cooler source regions, but those regions are only a few degrees cooler. Like their counterpart park units along the southwest coast (SWAN, Southwest Alaska I&M Network), the coastal portions of the CAKN park units appear to be a generally sensitive area for temperature change.

Figure 2.6 and Figure 2.7 show that the maritime influence does not extend very far inland in the vicinity of these park units, and rather rapidly gives way in winter to nearly full Arctic conditions, just to the north of the mountains draped by the Bagley Ice Field along the southern coast. Figure 2.8 and Figure 2.9 show the analogous summer situation. Generally, summer temperatures are warmer on the inland or interior side than along the south coast. Also, as expected, the highlands and mountains have lower maximums and somewhat lower minimums. The high sun and long days in mid-summer results in smaller spatial gradients and in considerably less temporal variability compared with winter. Cloudiness variations help control the amount of summer solar radiation absorbed.

The CAKN portion of Alaska has experienced the greatest individual daily extremes in the state's climate records. The interior can actually get hot, given its significant distance from any coastline, and Fort Yukon, 100 km downriver on the Yukon from YUCH, holds the state all-time record of +37.8°C, set on June 27, 1915. Similarly, the mountains and distance from the coast allow numerous cold pockets to form in winter. The all-time low for Alaska of –62.2°C was set at Prospect Creek Camp (along the Alaska Pipeline about 20 miles north of the Arctic Circle) on January 23, 1971. This range of 100.0°C is just shy of the largest of the 50 states, the 103.8 °C temperature range experienced in the state of Montana (-56.7 to +47.2 °C). Both Alaska sites are just a short distance north of YUCH. The North American low temperature record of -63 °C was set about 25 km east of the northeast corner of WRST, on February 3, 1947, at the airstrip at Snag, Yukon Territory, a small community of about 10 people with an official thermometer. This frigid air, originating in the northeast side of WRST near Mount Churchill, drains northeastward down the valley of the White River toward Snag, one of the very few instances where the United States supplies cold air to Canada. The Wrangells, St. Elias, and Chugach Ranges block the intrusion of mild Pacific air to this area. Fairbanks recorded a temperature of –52.2 °C and averages about 11 days a year with a minimum temperature of –40 °C or colder, a number that has ranged from 0 to 37 days for different winters. Northway temperature has reached –57.8 °C, and averages 19 days with –40 °C or colder, a number that has ranged from 0 to 46 days in a winter. They have averaged –38.5 °C for a month at a time.

The combination of heavy precipitation and cold temperatures results in phenomenal amounts of snow. Coastal Yakutat averages about 460 cm of snowfall and has seen as much as 1024 cm in 1975-76. Formerly a location with highly reliable and accurate snow data, Yakutat shows significant snow measurement problems from 1997-98 to 2002-03. The degradation of the United States snowfall records is an ongoing source of much concern (Kunkel et al. 2006). Valdez averages 749 cm of snow, has recorded 1133 cm in a single year, and has seen as much as 457 cm of snow in a single month. Nearby Thompson Pass just outside Valdez holds the official Alaska state record for seasonal snowfall, averaging 1402 cm per year. They also have the single snowiest winter, with 2475 cm in the winter of 1952-53, and a 24-hour total of 157.5 cm on December 29, 1955.

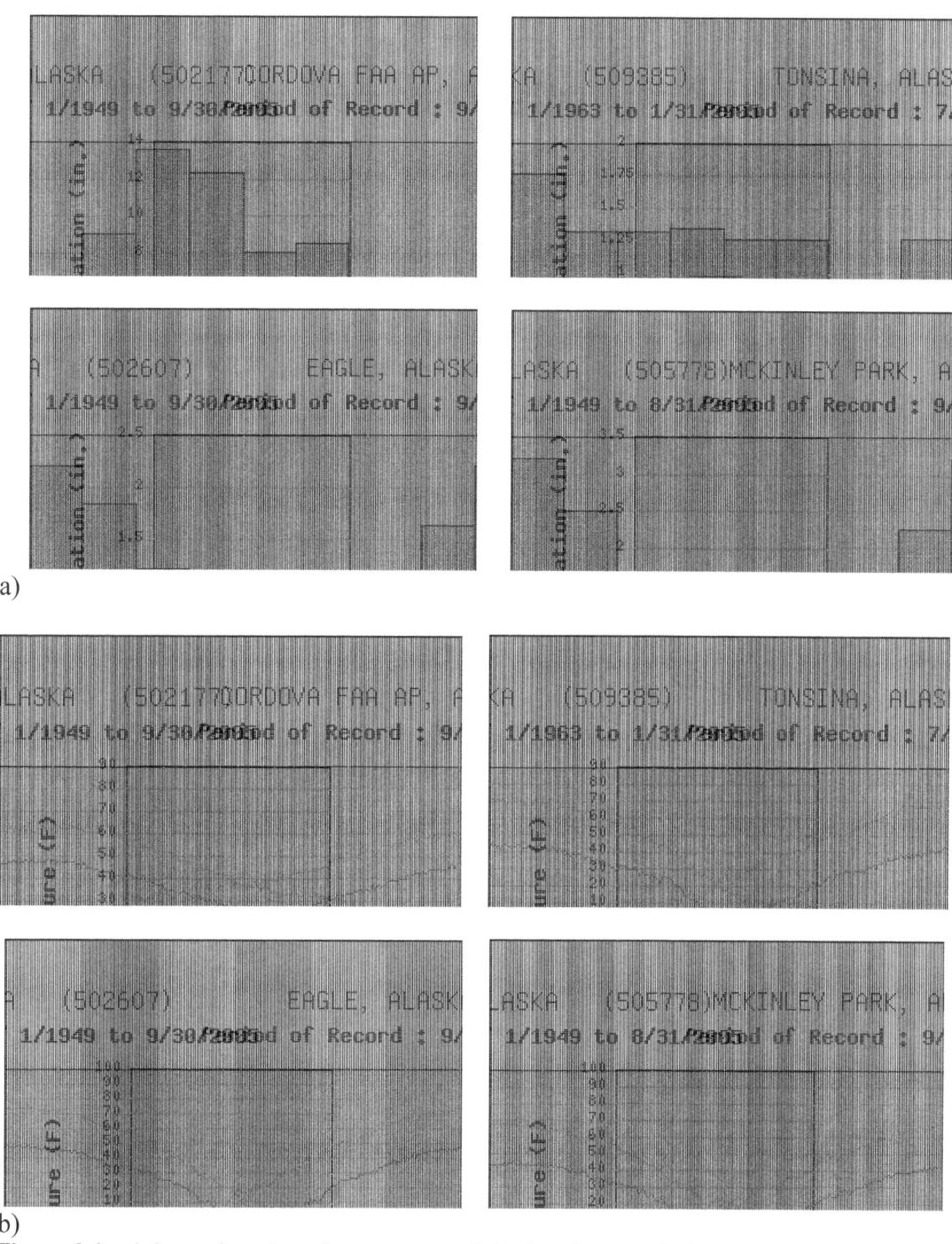

a)

b)

Figure 2.1. a) Annual cycles of average precipitation, by month, for CAKN parks. Differing scales. The intent of this figure is to show the shapes of the annual cycle rather than the amounts. b) Annual cycles of daily maximum and minimum temperature. Varying periods of record. Taken from the Western Regional Climate Center's Alaska historical data web pages at www.wrcc.dri.edu/summary/climsmak.html.

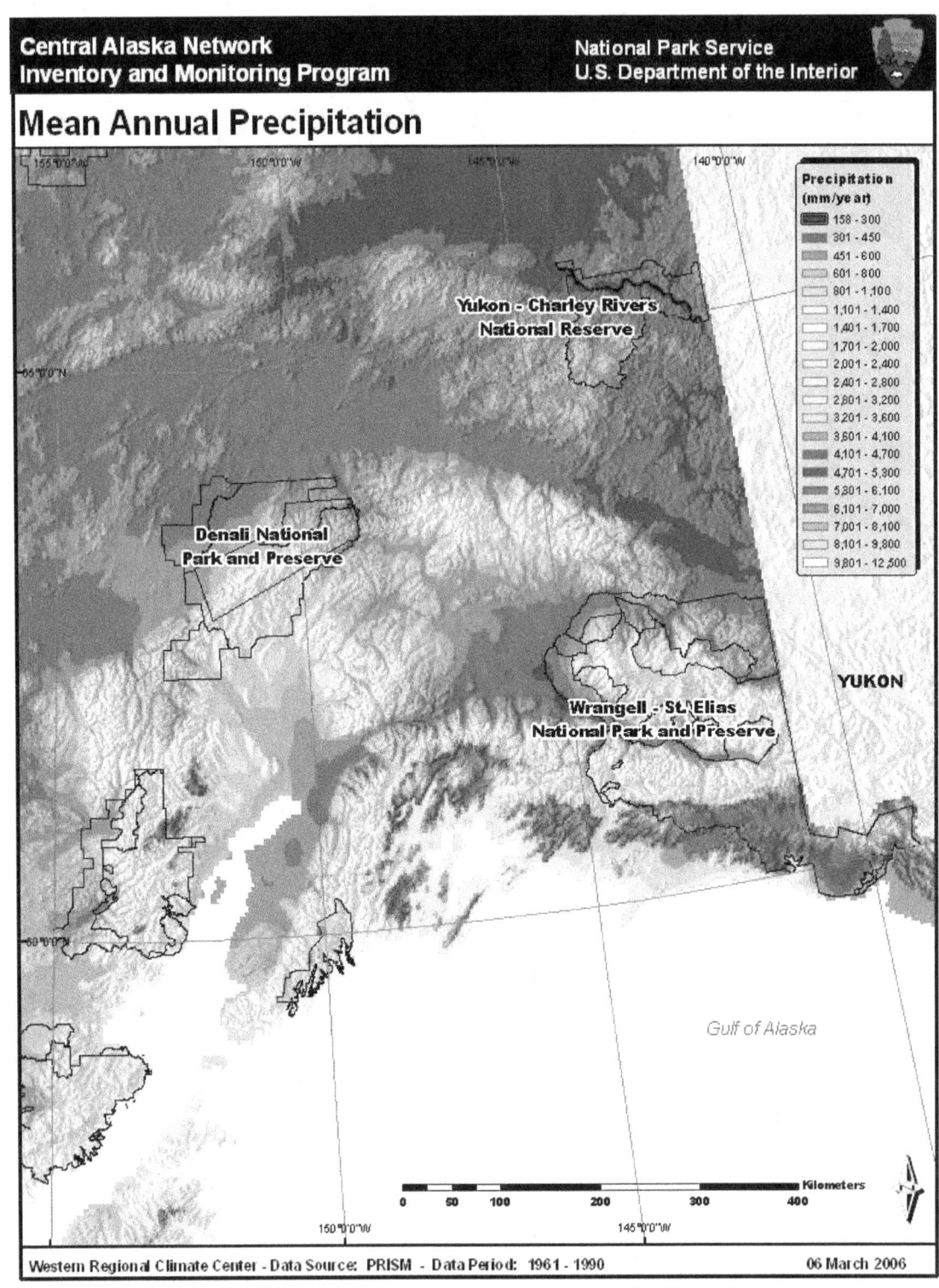

Figure 2.2. Mean annual precipitation, 1961–1990, within the CAKN region.

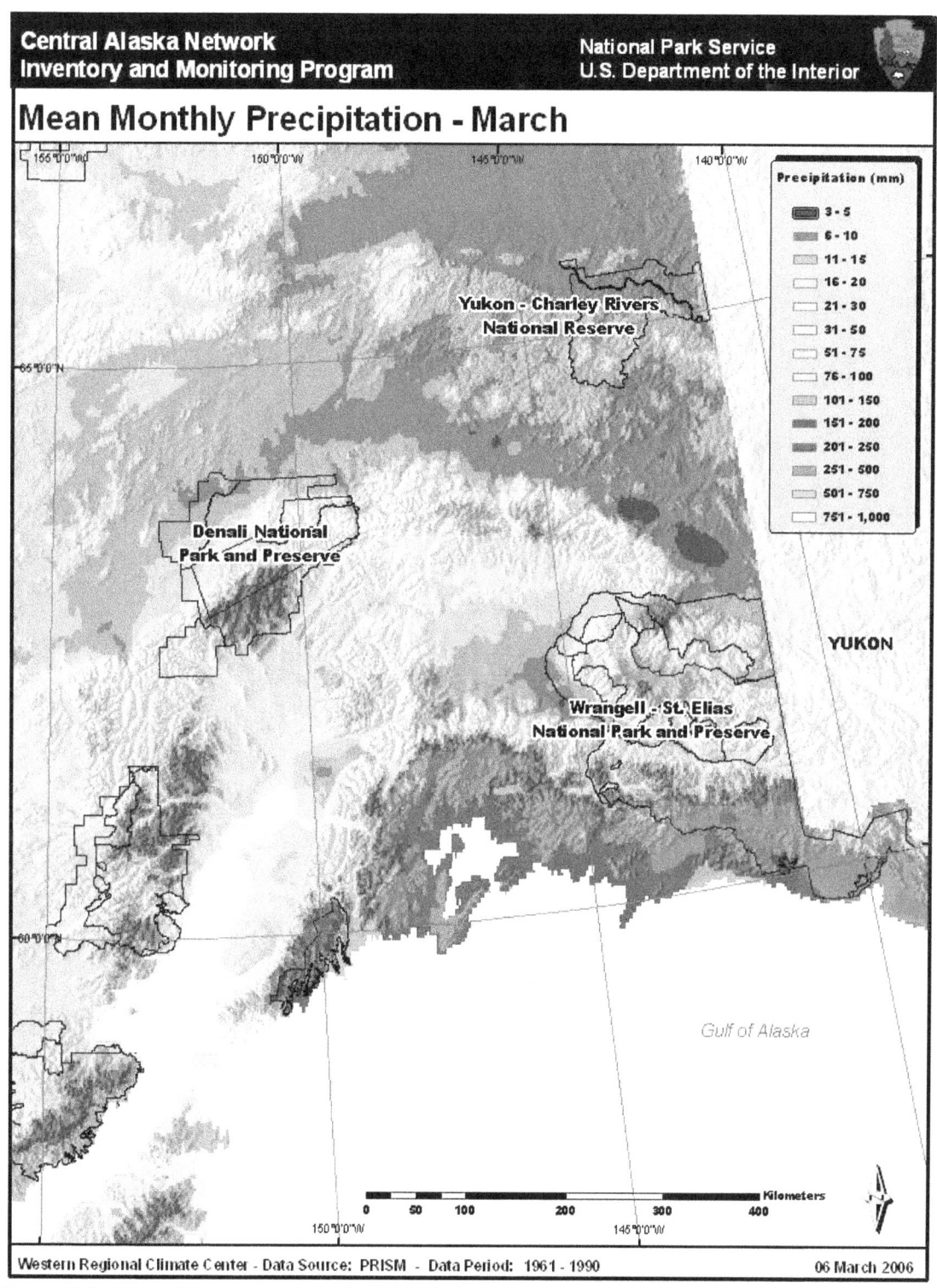

Mean Monthly Precipitation - March

Precipitation (mm)

- 3 - 5
- 6 - 10
- 11 - 15
- 16 - 20
- 21 - 30
- 31 - 50
- 51 - 75
- 76 - 100
- 101 - 150
- 151 - 200
- 201 - 250
- 251 - 500
- 501 - 750
- 751 - 1,000

Yukon - Charley Rivers
National Reserve

Denali National
Park and Preserve

YUKON

Wrangell - St. Elias
National Park and Preserve

Gulf of Alaska

Kilometers
0   50   100   200   300   400

Western Regional Climate Center - Data Source: PRISM - Data Period: 1961 - 1990   06 March 2006

Figure 2.3. Mean March precipitation, 1961–1990, within the CAKN region.

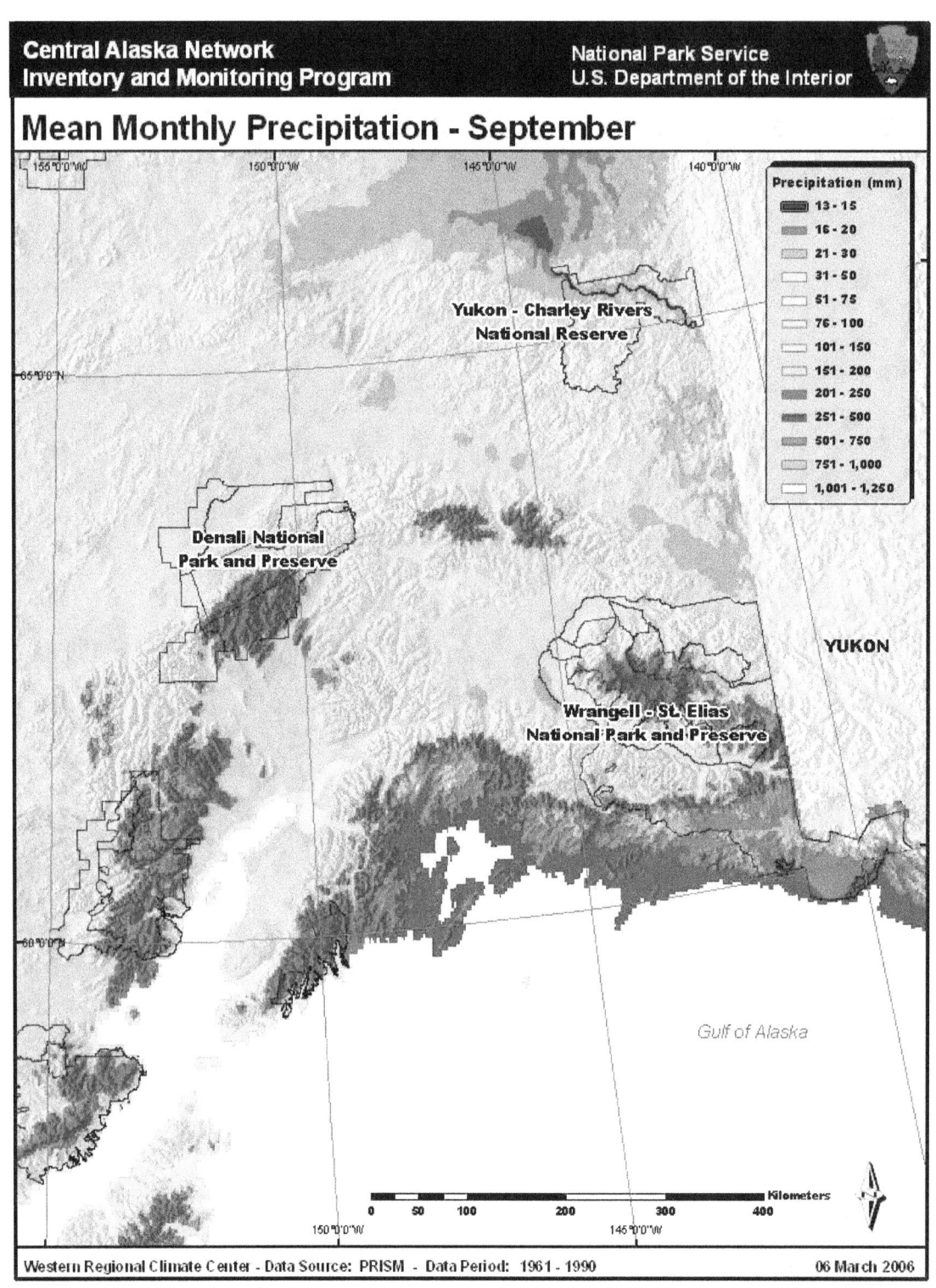

Mean Monthly Precipitation - September

Precipitation (mm)
13 - 15
16 - 20
21 - 30
31 - 50
51 - 75
76 - 100
101 - 150
151 - 200
201 - 250
251 - 500
501 - 750
751 - 1,000
1,001 - 1,250

Yukon - Charley Rivers
National Reserve

Denali National
Park and Preserve

YUKON

Wrangell - St. Elias
National Park and Preserve

Gulf of Alaska

Kilometers
0   50   100   200   300   400

Western Regional Climate Center - Data Source: PRISM - Data Period: 1961 - 1990   06 March 2006

Figure 2.4. Mean September precipitation, 1961–1990, within the CAKN region.

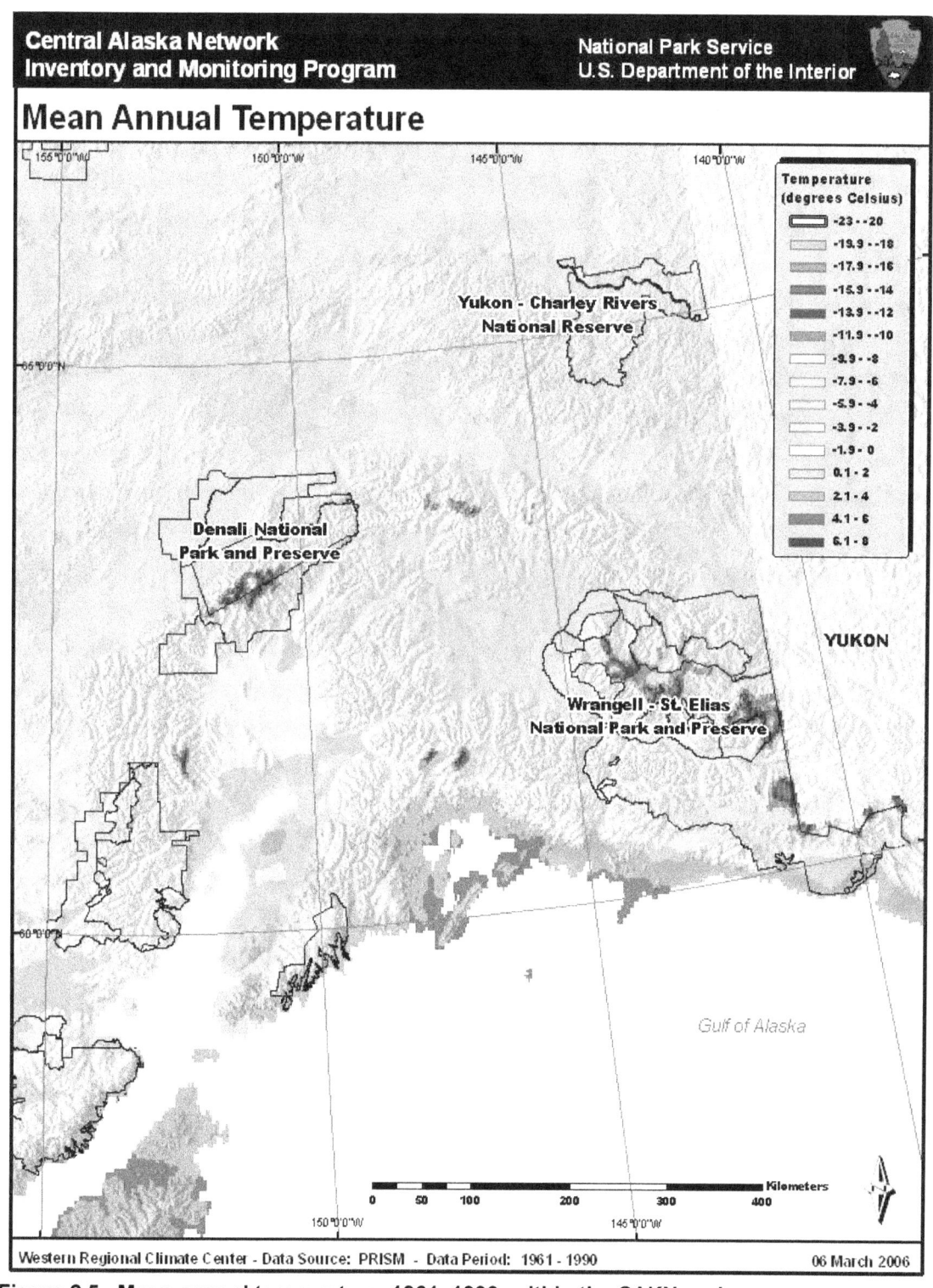

Mean Annual Temperature

Temperature
(degrees Celsius)
-23 - -20
-19.9 - -18
-17.9 - -16
-15.9 - -14
-13.9 - -12
-11.9 - -10
-9.9 - -8
-7.9 - -6
-5.9 - -4
-3.9 - -2
-1.9 - 0
0.1 - 2
2.1 - 4
4.1 - 6
6.1 - 8

Yukon - Charley Rivers
National Reserve

Denali National
Park and Preserve

YUKON

Wrangell - St. Elias
National Park and Preserve

Gulf of Alaska

Kilometers
0   50   100   200   300   400

Western Regional Climate Center - Data Source: PRISM - Data Period: 1961 - 1990   06 March 2006

Figure 2.5. Mean annual temperature, 1961–1990, within the CAKN region.

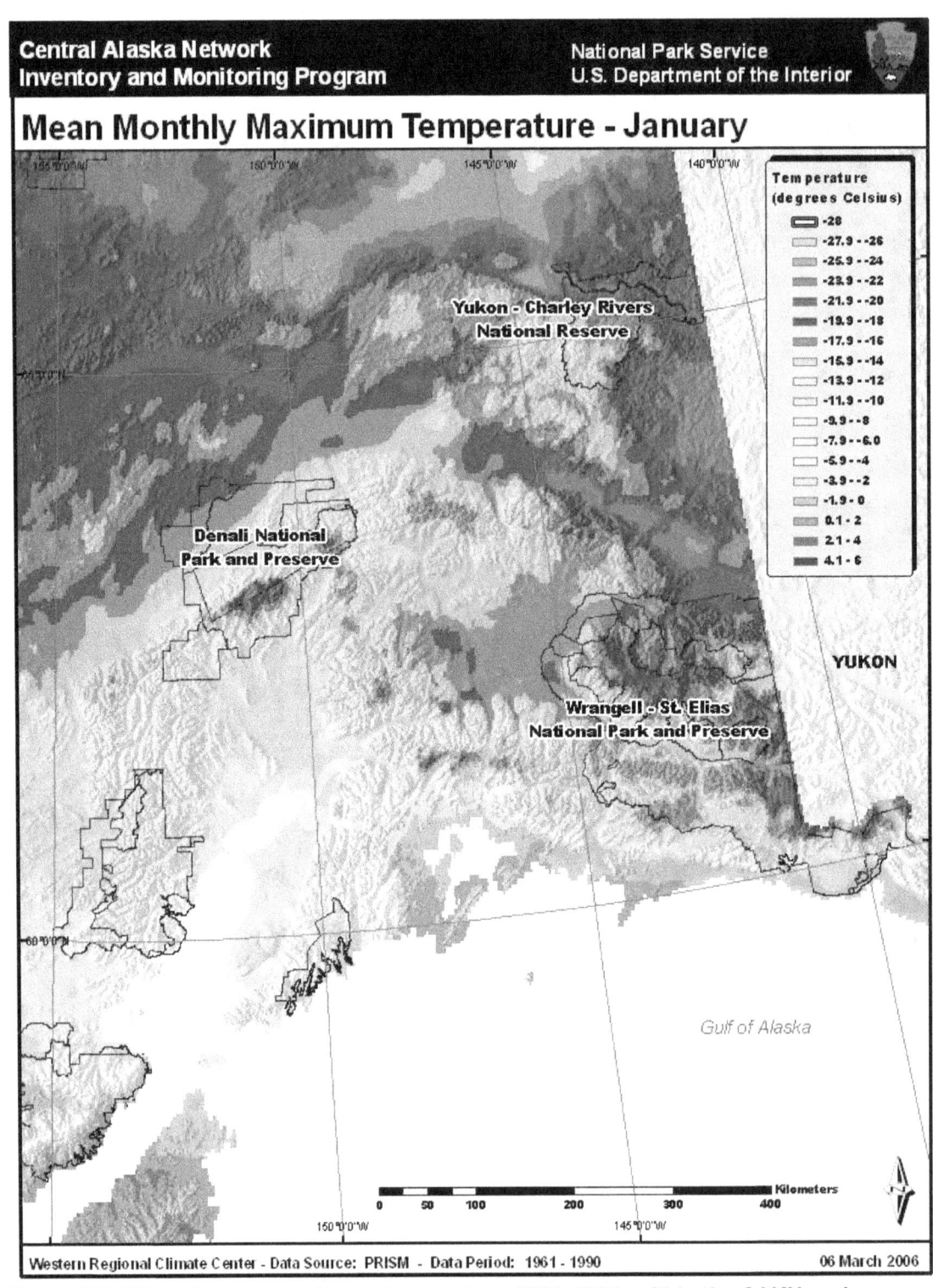

Figure 2.6. Mean January maximum temperature, 1961–1990, within the CAKN region.

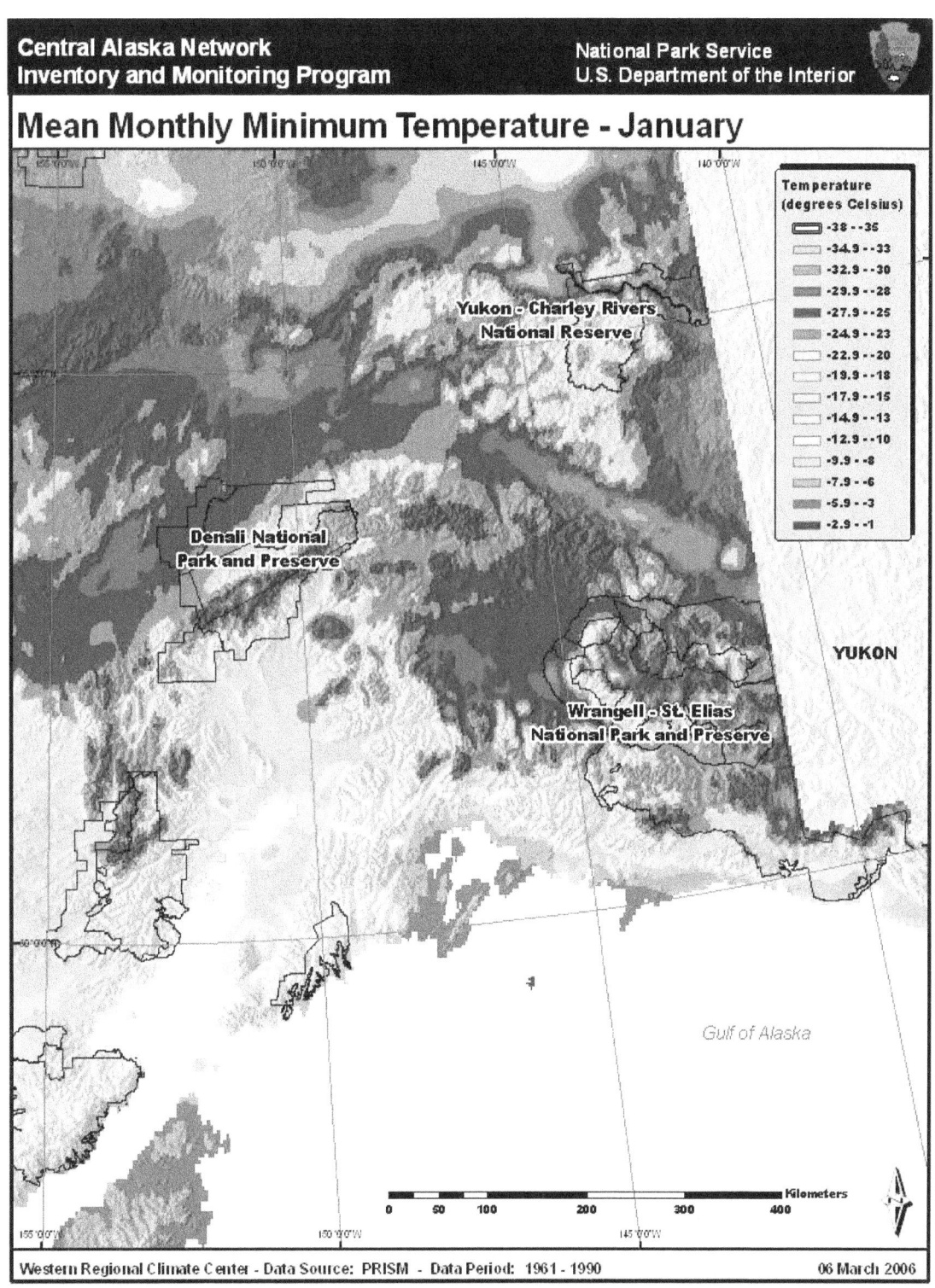

Figure 2.7. Mean January minimum temperature, 1961–1990, within the CAKN region.

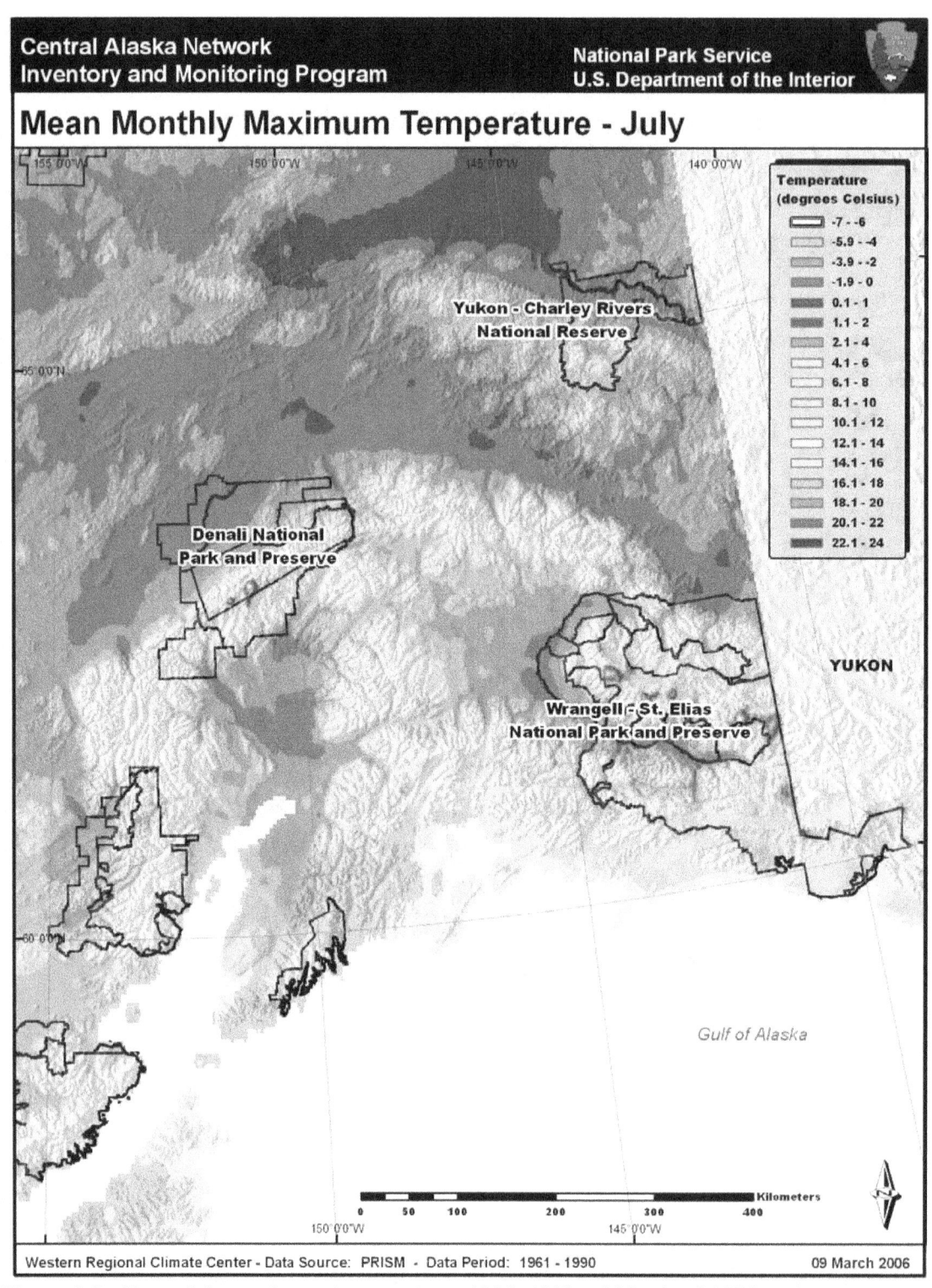

Figure 2.8. Mean July maximum temperature, 1961–1990, within the CAKN region.

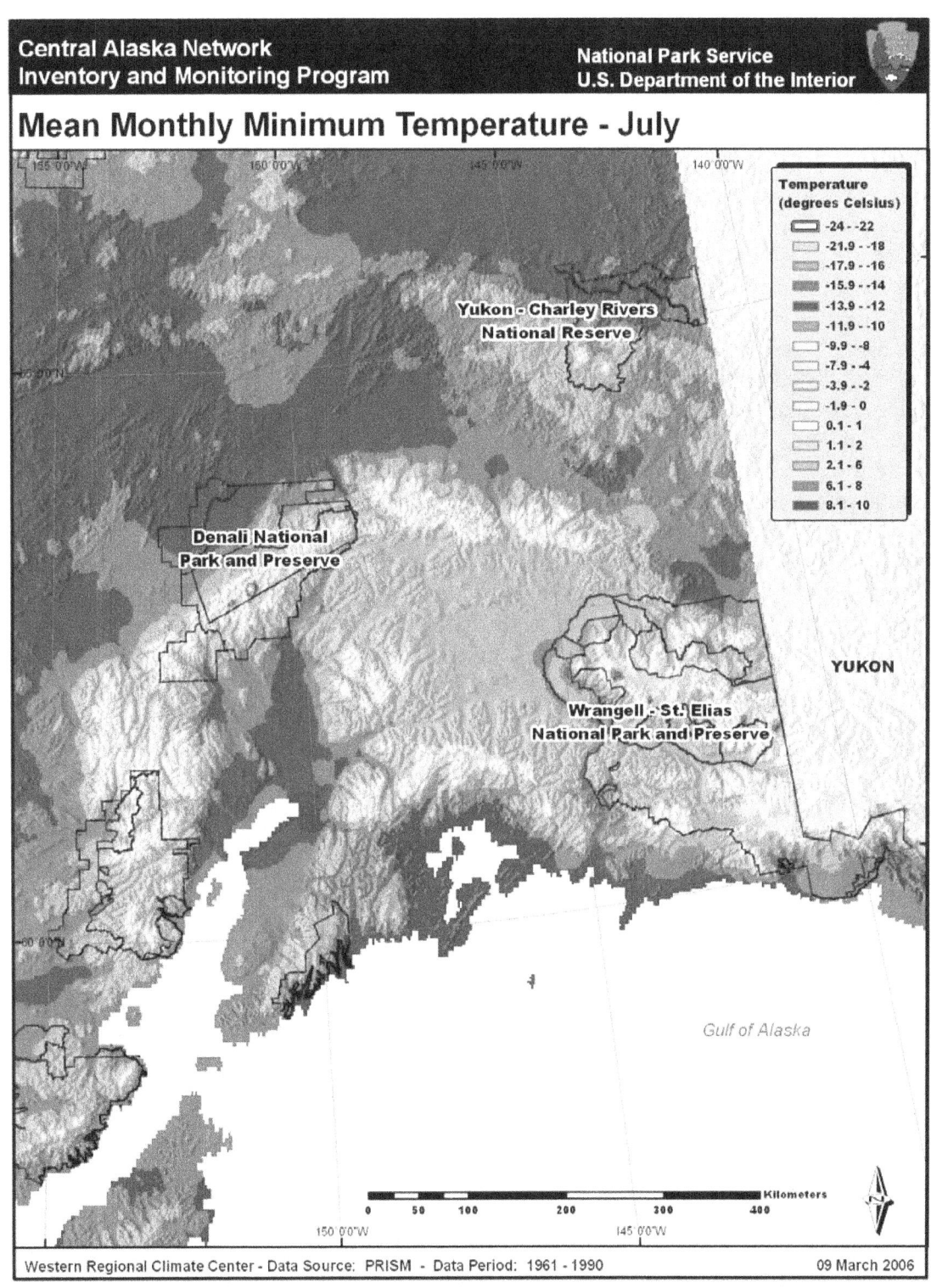

Figure 2.9. Mean July minimum temperature, 1961–1990, within the CAKN region.

2.2 Temporal Variability

Climate constantly fluctuates on a variety of temporal scales, and the CAKN area is no exception. . In addition, portions of the CAKN area experience two additional sources of variability that deserve comment.

The first of these involves variations in fields of atmospheric wind and pressure and of oceanic temperature and currents in the North Pacific Ocean south of the southern Alaska coastline. A single variation is thought to take 50-60 years to undergo a full "oscillation" from one phase and then back again (it is not yet clear if this is really a true oscillation, because we have witnessed only a portion of two cycles). The behavior was originally described by Mantua et al. (1997) who referred to it as the Pacific Decadal Oscillation (PDO). Effects of the PDO are greatest near the coast and diminish rapidly inland to the north of the coastal mountains. The cause of this variability is thought to relate to El Niño, La Niña, and the Southern Oscillation ("ENSO"), seen in the tropical Pacific far south of here. These variations, experienced during the winter half of the year, have major effects on the regional climate, the ocean circulation, and on biological organisms and populations, such as salmon (Mantua et al. 1997).

Secondly, in recent years, much of Alaska has experienced unusually mild winters, and temperatures during the 1990s rose substantially beyond those in previous decades. In many quarters, these are being taken as the harbinger of large scale planetary warming of the surface of the earth. The Arctic has long been expected to be the place where the signal would be seen soonest and most clearly, and many are interpreting the recent unusual warmth in that context (Arctic Climate Impact Assessment 2004). Areas along the south coast appear to be less affected than areas inland to the north, with the effects becoming more pronounced in the northern portions of DENA and YUCH. Thus, as with much of Alaska there are compelling reasons for much better knowledge of the variations of climate in this area.

Figure 2.9 shows temperature trends for different seasons at the 850 mb pressure level (1500 m altitude) from the NCEP Reanalysis (NCEP - National Centers for Environmental Prediction) since 1948. There is a clear tendency for warmer temperatures in recent portions of these records. There is a possibility of some contribution to this warming from long-term climate variations in the North Pacific (the PDO, discussed above, and its approximate 50-year time scale). There is in addition no agreement whether such variations are completely natural or could be enhanced by climate change. (The atmosphere may respond to warming by "choosing" certain preferred circulation patterns.) Whether this "oscillation" will reverse, or will otherwise continue to be a factor, and what is driving it, is a subject of much speculation and active research.

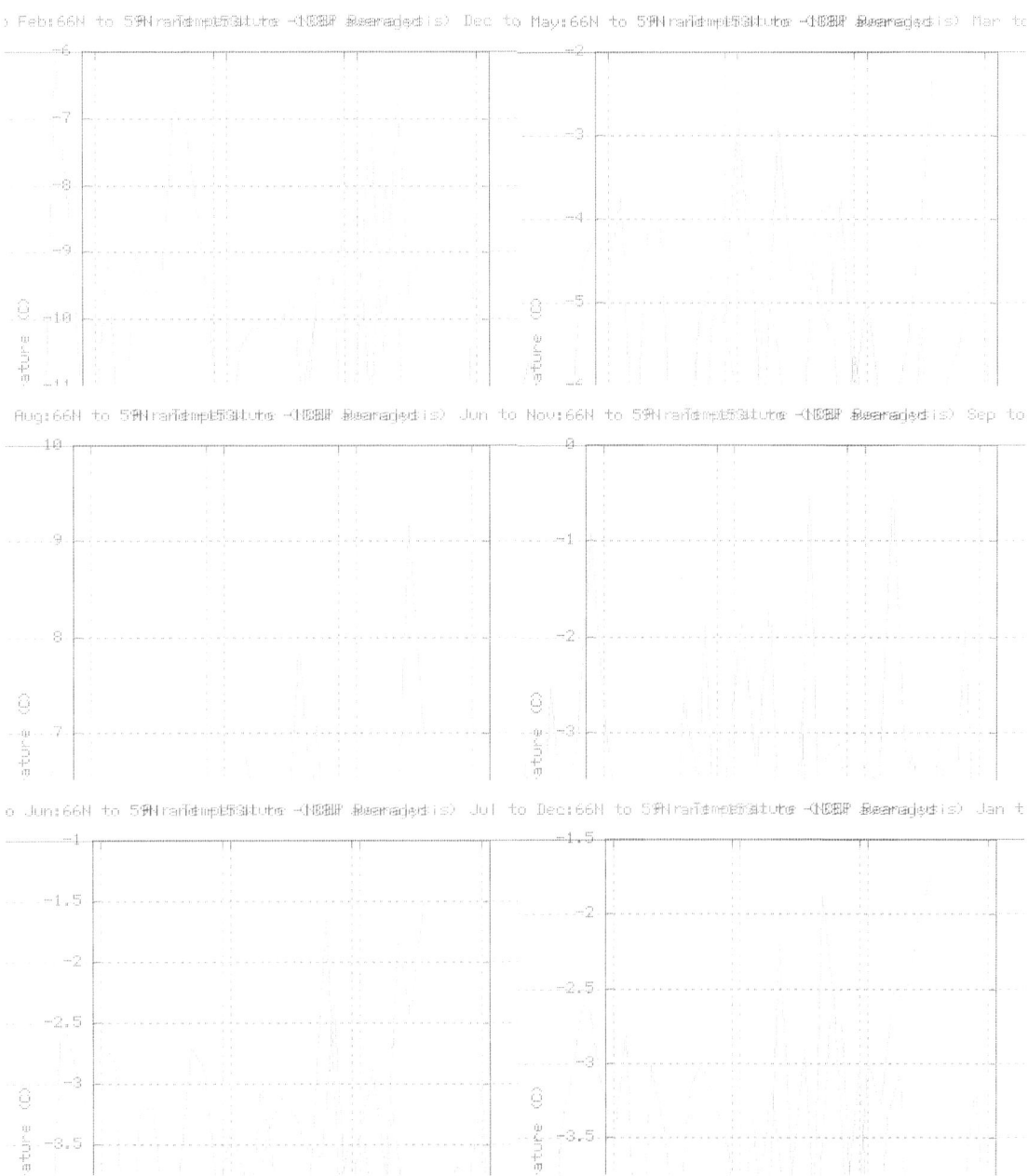

Figure 2.10. Area weighted temperature time series from NCEP Reanalysis at 850 mb for the lat-lon box [57-61 degrees North latitude] x [149-158 degrees West longitude]. Top left: Winter, Dec-Jan-Feb. Top right: Spring, Mar-Apr-May. Middle left: Summer, Jun-Jul-Aug. Middle right: Autumn, Sep-Oct-Nov. Bottom left: Annual winter-centered, July-thru-June. Bottom right: Annual calendar, Jan-thru-Dec. Data from 1948 through November 2005. Analysis software courtesy NOAA Climate Diagnostics Center.

3.0 Methods

Having discussed the climatic characteristics of CAKN, we now present the procedures that were used to obtain information for weather/climate stations within CAKN. This information was obtained from various sources, as mentioned in the following paragraphs. Retrieval of station metadata constituted a major component of this work.

3.1 Metadata Retrieval

A key component of station inventories is determining the kinds of observations that have been conducted over time, by whom, and in what manner; when each type of observation began; and whether these observations are still being conducted. Metadata about the observational process generally consist of a series of vignettes that apply to time intervals and, therefore, constitute a *history* rather than a single snapshot. This report has relied on metadata records from three sources: (a) Western Regional Climate Center (WRCC), (b) NPS personnel, and (c) other knowledgeable personnel, such as state climate office staff. Metadata (Table 3.1) have been obtained for weather/climate stations in and near the park units within CAKN. In this case "near" is typically 40-60 km, enough to include some key climate stations in data-sparse areas. An expanded list of relevant metadata fields for this inventory is provided in Appendix D.

Table 3.1. Primary metadata fields with explanations, as appropriate, for the inventory of weather/ climate stations within CAKN.

Metadata Field	Notes
Station name	Station name associated with network listed in "Climate Network."
Latitude	Numerical value (units: see coordinate units).
Longitude	Numerical value (units: see coordinate units).
Coordinate units	Latitude/longitude (units: decimal degrees, degree-minute-second, etc.).
Datum	Datum used as basis for coordinates: WGS 84, NAD 83, etc.
Elevation	Elevation of station above mean sea level (m).
Slope	Slope of ground surface below station (degrees).
Aspect	Azimuth that ground surface below station faces.
Climate division	NOAA climate division where station is located. Climate divisions are NOAA-specified zones sharing similar climate and hydrology characteristics.
Country	Country where station is located.
State	State where station is located.
County	County where station is located.
Weather/climate network	Primary weather/climate network the station belongs to (RAWS, Clean Air Status and Trends Network [CASTNet], etc.).
NPS unit code	Four-letter code identifying park unit where station resides.
NPS unit name	Full name of park unit.
NPS unit type	National park, national monument, etc.
UTM zone	If UTM (Coordinated Universal Time) is the only coordinate system available.
Location notes	Useful information not already included in "station narrative."
Climate variables	Temperature, precipitation, etc.

Metadata Field	Notes
Installation date	Date of station installation.
Removal date	Date of station removal.
Station photograph	Digital image of station.
Photograph date	Date photograph was taken.
Photographer	Name of person who took the photograph.
Station narrative	Anything related to general site description; may include site exposure, characteristics of surrounding vegetation, driving directions, etc.
Contact name	Name of the person involved with station operation.
Organization	Group or agency affiliation of contact person.
Contact type	Designation that identifies contact person as the station owner, observer, maintenance person, data manager, etc.
Position/job title	Official position/job title of contact person.
Address	Address of contact person.
E-mail address	E-mail address of contact person.
Phone	Phone number of contact person (and extension if available).
Contact notes	Other information needed to reach contact person.

The initial source of metadata for this report is metadata already stored at WRCC. This regional climate center acts as a working repository of many western climate records, including the main networks outlined in this section. Live and periodic ingests from all major national and western weather/climate networks are maintained at WRCC. These networks include the COOP network, Surface Airways Observation Program (SAO) networks jointly operated by NOAA and the Federal Aviation Administration (FAA), the NOAA upper-air observation network, NOAA data buoys, the RAWS network, the SNOTEL network, and various smaller networks. The WRCC is expanding its capability to ingest information from other networks as resources permit and usefulness dictates. This center has relied heavily on historic archives (in many cases supplemented with live ingests) to assess the quantity (not necessarily quality) of data available for NPS I&M network applications.

This report has relied primarily on metadata stored in the Applied Climate Information System (ACIS), a joint effort among regional climate centers (RCCs) and other NOAA entities. Metadata for the CAKN weather/climate stations that were identified from the ACIS database are available in an attached file (Appendix H). Historic metadata pertaining to major climate- and weather-observing systems in the United States are stored in ACIS where metadata are linked to the observed data. A distributed system, ACIS is synchronized among the RCCs. Mainstream software is utilized, including Postgress, Python™, and Java™ programming languages; CORBA®-compliant network software; and industry-standard, nonproprietary hardware and software. All major national climate and weather networks have been entered into the ACIS database. For this project, the available metadata from many smaller networks also have been entered. Data sets are in the NetCDF (Network Common Data Form) format, but the design allows for integration with legacy systems, including non-NetCDF files (used at WRCC) and additional metadata (added for this project). The ACIS also supports a suite of products to visualize or summarize data from these data sets. National climate-monitoring maps are updated daily using the ACIS data feed. The developmental phases of ACIS have utilized metadata supplied by the NCDC and NWS with many tens of thousands of entries, screened as well as possible for duplications, mistakes, and omissions.

CAKN personnel have compiled similar records based in part on access to material available from various Alaska and national sources, and in a circular fashion this sometimes includes records stored at WRCC, and within ACIS. ACIS records were cross-checked with records supplied by CAKN personnel. We have tried to eliminate duplicates, though some may remain. We have relied on local knowledge residing at the I&M network level as sources of information on additional specialized stations or small data networks.

We have also relied on information supplied at various times in the past by the Bureau of Land Management (BLM), NPS, NWS, NCDC and by personnel in the Alaska state climate offices in Anchorage and Fairbanks.

Two types of information have been used to complete the climate station inventory for CAKN.

- Station inventories: Information about the station-specific, operational procedures, latitude/longitude, elevation, measured elements, measurement frequency, sensor types, exposures, ground cover and vegetation, data-processing details, network, purpose, and managing individual or agency, etc. These are based on the metadata, without necessarily examining the data values.

- Data inventories: Information about measured data values, obtained from examination of the values themselves, including completeness, general quality, properties of data gaps, representation of missing data, flagging systems, how denotation of special circumstances in the data record, etc.

Extensive searches are typically required to develop historic station and data inventories. Both types of inventories frequently contain information gaps and often have built-in, unrealistic assumptions. Sources of information for these inventories frequently are difficult to recover or are undocumented and unreliable. In many cases, the actual weather/climate data available from different sources are not linked directly to metadata records. To the extent that actual data can be acquired (rather than just metadata), it is possible to cross-check these records and perform additional assessments based on the amount and completeness of the data.

Certain types of weather/climate networks that possess any of the following attributes have not been considered for inclusion in the inventory:

- Private networks with proprietary access and/or inability to obtain or provide sufficient metadata.
- Private weather enthusiasts (often with high-quality data) whose metadata are not available and whose data are not readily accessible.

28

- Unofficial observers supplying data to the NWS (lack of access to current data and historic archives; lack of metadata).
- Networks having no available historic data.
- Networks having poor-quality metadata.
- Networks having poor access to metadata.
- Real-time networks having poor access to real-time data.

Previous inventory efforts at WRCC have shown that for the weather networks identified in the preceding list, in light of the need for quality data to track weather and climate, the resources required and difficulty encountered in obtaining metadata or data are prohibitively large.

3.2 Criteria for Locating Stations

Stations do not have to be *inside* a park unit to be useful *for* that unit. In many cases, nearby stations have attributes that NPS stations (if even present) do not, including sufficient length, completeness, quality, or additional desired elements (e.g., wind, humidity, solar). Such stations can be very adequate for I&M needs, and without need for NPS expenditure. They can also offer very helpful backup and quality-control corroboration. However, reliance on others' stations creates a vested interest for NPS in working with the station owner to insure continued operation. We looked for all stations within a certain buffer distance of each park unit. These distances were generally 40-60 km, adjusted as necessary in some cases to be sure to include desired external stations.

The station locator maps presented in Chapter 4 were designed to show clearly the spatial distributions of all major weather/climate station networks in CAKN. We recognize that other mapping formats may be more suitable for other specific needs.

4.0 Station Inventory

Most weather and climate measurements are obtained from equipment that is part of a systematic network, usually supported by a single agency, and usually in support of some particular mission. Because of similar terminology, we will distinguish as needed between the weather/climate and I&M networks to forestall confusion.

Because idiosyncratic features of each weather/climate monitoring network can heavily affect interpretation of the data, the usual preference is to group weather stations by weather/climate network and combine results across networks with care.

4.1 Climate and Weather Networks

Most stations in the CAKN region are associated with at least one of ten major weather/climate networks (Table 4.1). Brief descriptions of each weather/climate network are provided below (see Appendix F for greater detail).

Table 4.1. Weather/Climate networks represented within CAKN.

Acronym	Name
CASTNet	Clean Air Status and Trends Network
COOP	NWS Cooperative Observer Program
GPMP	NPS Gaseous Pollutant Monitoring Program
LTEM	NPS Long-Term Environmental Monitoring
NADP	National Atmospheric Deposition Program
RAWS	Remote Automated Weather Station Network
SAO	NWS Surface Airways Observation Program
SNOTEL	USDA/NRCS Snowfall Telemetry Network
NRCS-SC	USDA/NRCS Snowcourse Network
NRCS-AM	USDA/NRCS Aerial Markers
Upper Air	NWS Upper Air Station
DENA-RC	Rock Creek special network run by DENA I&M Program
Canadian	Canadian climate station

4.1.1 Clean Air Status and Trends Network (CASTNet)

CASTNet is primarily an air-quality monitoring network managed by the EPA. Standard hourly weather and climate elements are measured and include temperature, wind, humidity, solar radiation, soil temperature, and sometimes moisture. These elements are intended to support interpretation of air-quality parameters that also are measured at CASTNet sites. Data records at CASTNet sites are generally one–two decades in length.

4.1.2 NWS Cooperative Observer Program (COOP)

30

The COOP network has been a foundation of the U.S. climate program for decades and continues to play an important role. Manual measurements are made by volunteers and consist of daily maximum and minimum temperatures, observation-time temperature, daily precipitation, daily snowfall, and snow depth. When blended with NWS measurements, the data set is known as SOD, or "Summary of the Day." The quality of data from COOP sites ranges from excellent to modest.

4.1.3 NPS Gaseous Pollutant Monitoring Program (GPMP)

GPMP data consist of hourly meteorological data in support of pollutant monitoring (mainly ozone, continuously measured): temperature, wind, humidity, solar, precipitation, and surface wetness. These data are of high quality, with records extending up to 1-2 decades length.

4.1.4 National Atmospheric Deposition Program (NADP)

This is a multi-agency network that provides data on precipitation, wet and dry deposition, and some other chemical species. Measurements are weekly to daily, often with a lag in reporting. Records generally extend over 1-2 decades.

4.1.5 Remote Automated Weather Station Network (RAWS)

The RAWS network is administered through many land management agencies, particularly the BLM and the Forest Service. Hourly meteorology elements are measured and include temperature, wind, humidity, solar radiation, barometric pressure, fuel temperature, and precipitation (when temperatures are above freezing). The fire community is the primary client for RAWS data. These sites are remote and data typically are transmitted via GOES (Geostationary Operational Environmental Satellite). Some sites operate all winter. Most data records for RAWS sites began during or after the mid-1980s.

4.1.6 NWS Surface Airways Observation Program (SAO)

These stations are located usually at major airports and military bases. Almost all SAO sites are automated. The hourly data measured at these sites include temperature, precipitation, humidity, wind, pressure, sky cover, ceiling, visibility, and current weather. Most data records begin during or after the 1940s, and these data are generally of high quality.

4.1.7 USDA/NRCS Snowfall Telemetry (SNOTEL) Network

The USDA/NRCS maintains a network of automated snow-monitoring stations known as SNOTEL. The network was implemented originally to measure daily precipitation and snow water content. Many modern SNOTEL sites now record hourly data, with many sites now recording temperature and snow depth. Most data records began during or after the mid-1970s.

4.1.8 USDA/NRCS Snowcourse Network (SC)

The USDA/NRCS maintains another network of snow-monitoring stations in addition to SNOTEL. These sites are known as snowcourses. Some of these SC sites are read by airplane through the use of aerial markers and are referred to as NRCS-AM sites in this report. These are all manual sites, measuring only snow depth and snow water content one or two times per month during the months of January to June. Data records for these snowcourses often extend back to the 1920s or 1930s, and the data are generally of high quality. Many of these sites have been replaced by SNOTEL sites, but several hundred snowcourses are still in operation.

4.1.9 Regional Network (I&M)

These stations are associated with the Denali Rock Creek network, which is a local dense network of 5-6 stations near DENA headquarters, part of the NPS Long Term Ecological Monitoring Program, or LTEM (Oakley and Boudreau 2000). Data consist of hourly temperature, wind, solar, and precipitation information, most of them recorded to data loggers, with a few sites converted to live reporting. Earliest records start in 1994.

4.1.10 Other Networks

Station metadata were obtained from two other sources in addition to the above weather/climate networks. First, metadata for a Canadian weather/climate station were available near the eastern boundary of WRST. Second, station metadata were obtained from the NOAA upper air dataset. These are twice-a-day soundings that use balloons to sample the atmospheric column with a vertical resolution of 10 m or less, at 0000 and 1200 GMT. Measured elements include temperature, pressure, height, wind speed and direction. These are free-air properties, at a mixture of fixed (mandatory) and variable levels, and are our only source of long-term vertical information of good quality. Records are typically 3-6 decades in length, and can be used for many kinds of climate studies.

4.2 Station Locations

One objective of this report is to show the locations of weather and climate stations for the CAKN region, in relation to the outer boundaries of the NPS park units of the CAKN region. A station does not have to be within the park boundaries to provide useful data and information regarding the park unit in question. Because of logistical reasons the major weather/climate networks in the CAKN have in general only a few stations in or near each park unit (Table 4.2). In the separate park unit descriptions we select for further discussion a few stations expected to be of special interest.

Table 4.2. Number of stations in or near CAKN (listed by park unit and weather/climate network).

Denali National Park and Preserve (DENA)	
Weather/Climate Network	**Number of Stations**
CASTNet	1
COOP	5
GPMP	1
NADP	1
RAWS	14
SNOTEL	1
NRCS-AM, NRCS-SC	14
Upper Air	3
Wrangell-St. Elias National Park and Preserve (WRST)	
COOP	14
RAWS	15
SAO	4
NRCS-AM, NRCS-SC	23
Upper Air	2
Yukon-Charley Rivers National Preserve (YUCH)	
COOP	2
RAWS	5
SAO	1
NRCS-AM, NRCS-SC	8

4.2.1. Denali National Park and Preserve (DENA)

The main physical influence, the Alaska Range, separates the maritime influence on the south from the continental interior influence on the north. The station density and distribution in DENA (Figure 4.1) is beginning to improve, and in general the Alaska Range is approximately encircled by a set of stations in the lowlands to the north and south. A SNOTEL station was recently (28 July 2005) installed at Kantishna (without snow water equivalent) and seems to be working well, providing hourly data. Stations of this type are well-suited to the conditions experienced here, have a proven track record, and can record precipitation data reliably in very demanding conditions. RAWS sites are found both near the access road and at remote locations, and more were recently installed near the access road by the I&M program in summer 2005. These seemed to have worked rather well during their first winter, with very little data loss. RAWS stations are good candidates for locations where accurate all-year precipitation measurements are not needed, and where snow will not bury the station. The McKinley River RAWS site provided hourly snow depth data during the winter of 2005-06 with no major data corruption, a very commendable result. The south side of the Alaska Range does not have quite as good coverage, especially for precipitation, though the logistics are more difficult.

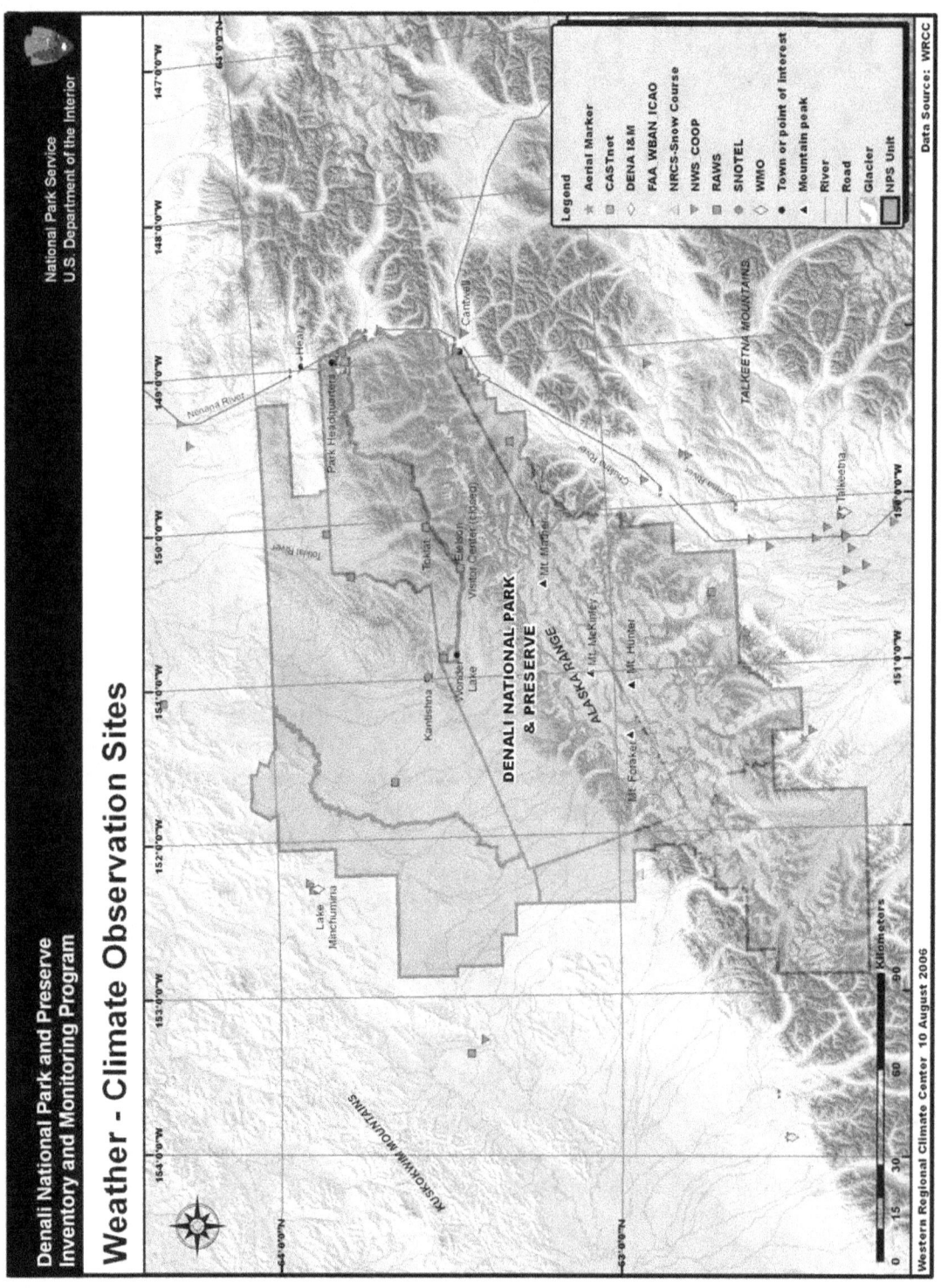

Figure 4.1. Station locations for DENA.

34

Several NWS stations in the COOP network can be found in or near DENA. NWS records indicate a COOP station starting at Healy in 1938, but we have unable to locate data from this site through NCDC archives in order to check the metadata. The main metadata record for this station indicates a start date of November 1976, and there is no indication in NOAA metadata records that the site has closed. However, we have received no data from the site (50-3581) since January 2005.

The McKinley Park NWS COOP site starts on 7 Dec 1922 and appears to have the longest record in the vicinity of DENA. WRCC daily data from this station start in 1949. The station has been moved around in the area, and we have not yet established with certainty that this station actually provides a homogeneous and continuous record of climate for the entire time. The site has had a similar elevation since summer 1925, which is encouraging. After a long period of fairly complete data, records from the 1980s became more erratic, data completeness improved in the mid 1990s, and since the turn of the 21st Century there are a number of months with missing data.

Another NWS COOP station was located at Minchumina, on the northwest side of the nearby lake, from 1949 to spring of 1967. The RAWS site there appears to be about 1.7 km northwest of this COOP site, 16 meters higher, north of the landing strip and no closer than about 1 km from the water. The RAWS record is short (June 1992 onward) but is nevertheless accumulating.

The Ruth Glacier RAWS site is more sporadic, and did not report in real-time over the winter of 2005-06. This site is actually about 500 m above the Ruth River on a southwest spur of the Tokosha Mountains. A full SNOTEL site would be worthy of consideration on the south side of the Alaska Range near the projected terminus of one of the major glaciers, because such stations supply relatively unique information.

As noted in Section 4.1.9, the DENA I&M Program runs a small network of six stations near the entrance station. This site spans a range of elevations in the Rock Creek drainage. At least two of these are RAWS stations reporting through NIFC.

4.2.2. Wrangell-St. Elias National Park and Preserve (WRST)

WRST has tremendous topographic and climatic diversity and is huge, the largest single element in the national park system (5.3 million hectares, with adjoining Kluane National Park in Canada adding another 2.2 million). The remnant ice fields, extremely wet maritime sections, and bitterly cold interior locations provide a significant challenge for measurement. Consequently the density of stations is not high (Figure 4.2) and major climate zones are barely represented in the longer records.

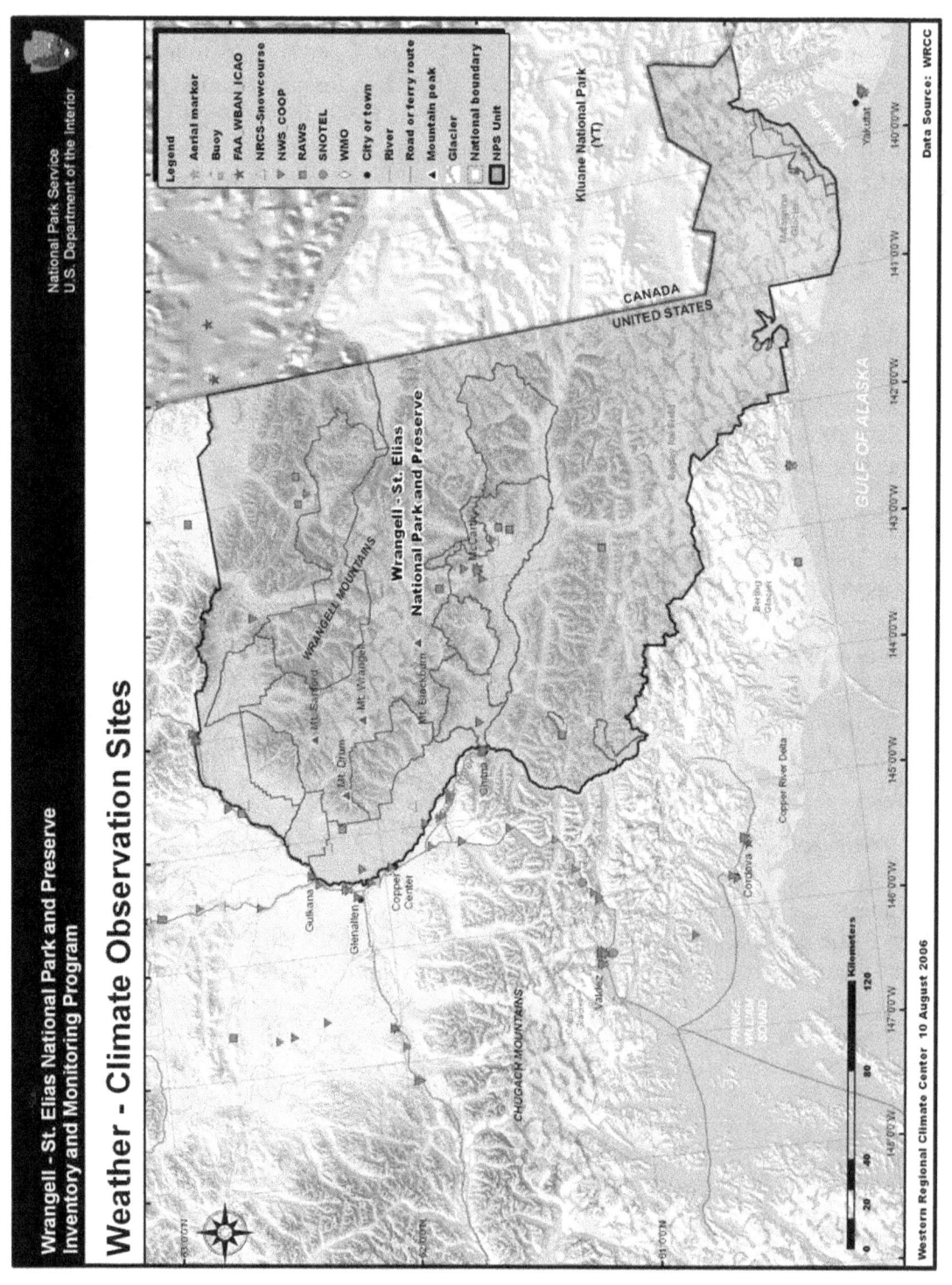

Figure 4.2. Station locations for WRST.

The mining town of McCarthy has had a climate station since 1968. Unfortunately it has wandered over three locations. Note that the NWS spelled the station "Mc Carthy" (this makes a difference) from 1968 to 1983, during which it also had two COOP ID numbers 50-5752 (1968-1976) and 50-5754 (1976-1983, and one minute of longitude east of and 20 meters lower than the previous location). From available records we cannot tell how far these were apart. (Other metadata show the first station may have started in 1949 or earlier, but the data at WRCC/NCDC begin in 1968.) The records are complete and appear very good from within each of the two periods. There is a gap from March to October 1983, at which time the current site (spelled "McCarthy" 3 SW) began (50-5757; 5.6 km WSW of the 2nd location and 88 m lower). This record also has only a few missing months. Curiously, all three sites show about 180 cm / 70 inches of snowfall, with period-mean precipitation ranging from 432 mm to 530 mm to 483 mm at the three respective sites, probably an accidental combination of site differences and climate variation (though the values are consistent with topographic features). With the significant topographic variation and local variability, this vignette shows that it is especially important that stations not move over periods of decades, if possible. These moves are likely due to observer issues.

The NWS COOP station at Nabesna (50-6147) shows a period of record from 1967, but operated from Oct 1967 thru Apr 1968 at one location, and then had a gap of a dozen years until August 1980, the same ID number, and a complete record until 1998 after which 8 scattered months are missing. This pattern of frequent missing data is seen at many NWS COOP sites nationwide starting in the 1990s, and has a complex origin.

A number of airport and NWS COOP stations have operated for many decades around the outer boundaries of WRST, especially to the north and west, and these records are of considerable value in supplementing measurement programs within the boundaries. Indeed they are going to be the only source of historical observations for these large acreages of sparse measurements. Likewise, the station at Yakutat has an excellent, complete and very valuable record extending back to at least July 1949 and updated daily by NWS. This site averages 3703 mm / 145.8 inches (1949-2005) of annual precipitation and in Sept-Oct of 1987 recorded 2467 mm / 97.14 inches of precipitation in 2 months.

4.2.3. Yukon-Charley Rivers National Preserve (YUCH)

Though a large area, YUCH nonetheless does not have the same degree of climatic and topographic diversity as WRST and DENA. Of the three CAKN park units, however, it has by far the lowest density of weather stations (Figure 4.3), with just a very few sites inside the boundary, and most of these dating from 2002 or later. The only measurement platform in YUCH that has operated for more than a decade is the RAWS site at Ben Creek, which started in 1990. During the last 16 years, this site had only three calendar years (1994, 1997, 2001) with data from every month of the year. During most winters there are a few missing months. This might be a testament to low solar angles, extreme cold, and perhaps occasionally, snow.

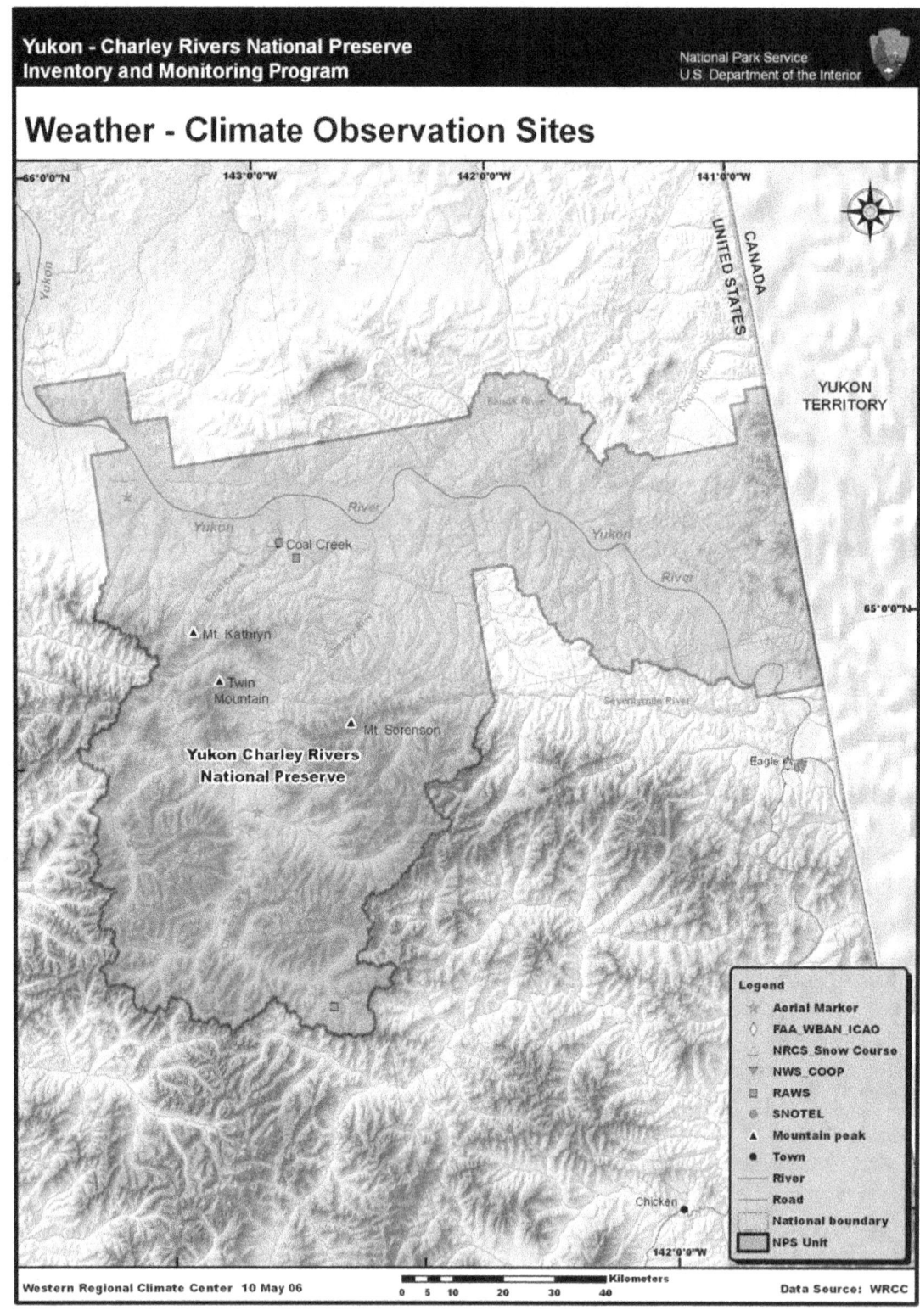

Figure 4.3. Station locations for YUCH.

Data transmitted via satellite from the new Coal Creek RAWS exhibited some very unusual behavior over the winter of 2005-06, apparently the result of a datalogger programming issue. This site was visited in late spring of 2006, and the downloaded data were found to be complete and in good shape. This illustrates the wisdom of a backup procedure at all such sites that results in the downloading of data directly during site visits, so that the full record can be restored, even if after the fact. It further illustrates that some care is needed to distinguish between the "live" data and subsequently acquired downloaded data, for example by using data flags. The Upper Charley RAWS appears to be providing good data when it is transmitting, but there are large gaps in the transmitted data.

The RAWS sites at Birch Creek (to the northwest) and Eagle (to the east) have similar major data gaps in records from winter. The RAWS station at Chicken had a short gap in the winter of 2005-06, but functioned well at -46°C, demonstrating the ability of these stations to function and report during extreme cold.

With such sparse and short records from within YUCH, there is especially more need for reliance on outside stations than other park units. Pam Sousanes, environmental specialist for CAKN, reported that NPS has relied on data from the NWS COOP station at Eagle for a long term climate perspective for YUCH. This station has a very long history, with metadata entries at NCDC dating to 1899. From September 1949 onward, data are available as a COOP station from NCDC/WRCC archives. The data record from the Eagle station has numerous gaps in the 1960's to early 1970s, and occasional missing months in the 1980s, but no missing months from about 1990 onward, and no month with more than 6 days of missing data. Chicken, to the southeast, was re-established in August 1996 as an NWS COOP station. Circle Hot Springs is the closest NWS COOP station to the northwest. Though its record extends from 1949, there is a long gap from the mid 1970s until 2000. From 2000 to present data from the station has been quite sporadic.

4.3 Sites and Metadata

Lists of stations have been compiled showing the various stations and sites in each of several main networks (Table 4.3). The information in these tables will also be available as digital files accompanying this printed report. A station does not have to be within the boundaries to provide useful data and information regarding the park unit in question. Some might be physically *within* the administrative or political boundaries, whereas others might be just outside, or even some distance away, but would be *nearby* in behavior and representativeness. In the CAKN area, the number of internal sites is relatively small, and the number of nearby stations is higher, though usually still not fully sufficient for all applications. What constitutes "useful" and "representative" varies according to application, type of element, period of record, procedural or methodological observation conventions, and the like.

Table 4.3. Weather/climate stations inside CAKN park units and within 40-60 km of their boundaries. Each listing includes station name, location, and elevation; weather/climate network associated with station; operational start/end dates for station; and whether station is located inside park boundaries.

Name	Lat.	Lon.	Elev. (m)	Network	Start	End	In Park?
Denali National Park and Preserve (DENA)							
McKinley Park	63.71953	-148.96567	631	COOP	1922	Present	YES
Rock Creek Forest	63.73149	-148.98238	737	DENA-RC	1995	Present	YES
Rock Creek Permafrost	63.72664	-148.97771	717	DENA-RC	1995	Present	YES
Rock Creek Treeline	63.73537	-149.00688	960	DENA-RC	1995	Present	YES
Rock Creek Upper	63.74671	-149.01453	1350	DENA-RC	1995	Present	YES
Trapper Creek	63.31830	-150.30060	146	GPMP	1998	2001	YES
Rock Creek Air Quality	63.72360	-148.96390	649	NADP	1980	Present	YES
Dunkle Hills	63.26823	-149.53887	844	NRCS-AM	2003	Present	YES
Eldridge	63.04683	-150.05627	994	NRCS-AM	2002	Present	YES
Kantishna	63.53845	-150.98365	509	NRCS-AM	1995	Present	YES
Upper W Fork Yentna	62.50929	-152.44913	293	NRCS-AM	2002	Present	YES
Rock Creek Bottom	63.72300	-148.96724	671	NRCS-SC	1993	Present	YES
Rock Creek Ridge	63.72631	-148.98683	786	NRCS-SC	1993	Present	YES
Stampede	63.74961	-150.32824	549	NRCS-SC	2002	Present	YES
Denali Visitor Center	63.73331	-148.90055	509	RAWS	2004	Present	YES
Dunkle Hills	63.26699	-149.54153	808	RAWS	2003	Present	YES
Eielson Visitor Center	63.43072	-150.31026	1202	RAWS	2005	Present	YES
McKinley River	63.65972	-151.63972	256	RAWS	1992	Present	YES
Rock Creek Lower	63.73505	-149.00911	987	RAWS	1995	Present	YES
Ruth Glacier	62.70996	-150.53984	1006	RAWS	1998	Present	YES
Stampede	63.74778	-150.32805	549	RAWS	2003	Present	YES
Toklat	63.52550	-150.04648	890	RAWS	2005	Present	YES
Wigand	63.81208	-150.04977	533	RAWS	2003	Present	YES
Wonder Lake	63.49000	-150.88000	646	RAWS	1995	Present	YES
Kantishna*	63.53845	-150.98365	509	SNOTEL	2005	Present	YES
Cantwell	63.40000	-148.90000	655	COOP	1983	Present	NO
Chulitna River Lodge	62.88333	-149.83333	381	COOP	1971	Present	NO
Healy 2 NW	63.88333	-149.01667	454	COOP	1976	Present	NO
Minchumina	63.88333	-152.28333	210	COOP	1949	1967	NO
Chelatna Lake	62.46456	-151.46103	503	NRCS-AM	1964	Present	NO
Dutch Hills	62.60516	-150.85509	945	NRCS-AM	1980	Present	NO
Nugget Bench	62.51782	-150.93996	613	NRCS-AM	1968	Present	NO
Ramsdyke Creek	62.61684	-150.80858	677	NRCS-AM	1980	Present	NO
Tokositna River	62.62942	-150.77578	259	NRCS-AM	1980	Present	NO
Minchumina	63.88705	-152.30276	223	NRCS-SC	1967	Present	NO

Name	Lat.	Lon.	Elev. (m)	Network	Start	End	In Park?
Purkey Pile	62.94543	-152.25745	617	NRCS-SC	1980	Present	NO
Farewell	63.72333	-154.07667	236	RAWS	1996	Present	NO
Minchumina	63.89333	-152.31056	226	RAWS	1992	Present	NO
Telida	63.44000	-153.35667	198	RAWS	1991	Present	NO
Wein Lake	64.31500	-151.08333	320	RAWS	1998	Present	NO
Anchorage	61.22000	-149.83000	51	Upper Air	1943	1953	NO
Anchorage	61.17000	-149.98000	29	Upper Air	1953	1964	NO
Anchorage	61.17000	-150.02000	45	Upper Air	1964	Present	NO
Fairbanks	61.83000	-147.72000	134	Upper Air	1937	1951	NO
Fairbanks	64.82000	-147.87000	135	Upper Air	1951	Present	NO
McGrath	62.97000	-155.62000	103	Upper Air	1942	Present	NO
Wrangell-St. Elias National Park and Preserve (WRST)							
Mc Carthy 1 NE	61.43333	-142.91667	488	COOP	1968	1976	YES
Mc Carthy 1 NE	61.43333	-142.90000	469	COOP	1976	1983	YES
McCarthy 3 SW	61.41667	-143.00000	381	COOP	1984	Present	YES
Nabesna	62.40000	-143.00000	884	COOP	1967	Present	YES
Long Glacier	61.82166	144.07982	1469	NRCS-AM	2004	Present	YES
Notch Airstrip	61.00562	141.53171	806	NRCS-AM	2005	Present	YES
Tebay	61.18095	144.33920	587	NRCS-AM	2004	Present	YES
Chisana	62.07194	-142.06528	1012	NRCS-SC	1993	Present	YES
Chokosna	61.46667	-143.83333	472	NRCS-SC	1993	Present	YES
Dadina Lake	61.85000	-144.81667	658	NRCS-SC	1985	Present	YES
Lost Creek	62.51667	-143.16667	920	NRCS-SC	1993	Present	YES
May Creek	61.34833	-142.69417	503	NRCS-SC	1993	Present	YES
Sanford River	62.21667	-145.06667	695	NRCS-SC	1967	Present	YES
Chicken Creek	62.12402	-141.84737	1597	RAWS	2004	Present	YES
Chisana	62.07750	-142.05000	1012	RAWS	1988	Present	YES
Chititu	61.27359	-142.62090	1385	RAWS	2004	Present	YES
Gates Peninsula	61.60289	-143.01321	1237	RAWS	2005	Present	YES
Klawasi	62.08056	-144.87083	945	RAWS	1991	Present	YES
May Creek	61.34806	-142.70389	503	RAWS	1990	Present	YES
Tana Knob	60.90800	-142.90131	1140	RAWS	2005	Present	YES
Tebay	61.18095	-144.33920	573	RAWS	2005	Present	YES
Beaver Creek	62.40000	-140.86667	649	Canadian	1968	Present	NO
Chisana	62.08333	-142.01639	968	COOP	1966	1972	NO
Chitina	61.51667	-144.43333	183	COOP	1950	1971	NO
Glennallen	62.11667	-145.53333	444	COOP	1965	2004	NO
Kenny Lake	61.73333	-144.93333	390	COOP	2000	Present	NO
Paxson	63.03333	-145.50000	823	COOP	1975	Present	NO
Slana	62.70000	-143.98333	668	COOP	1957	Present	NO

Name	Lat.	Lon.	Elev. (m)	Network	Start	End	In Park?
Snowshoe Lake	62.03333	-146.70000	701	COOP	1963	Present	NO
Tok	63.35000	-143.05000	494	COOP	1954	Present	NO
Tonsina	61.65000	-145.18333	457	COOP	1963	Present	NO
Valdez	61.08000	-146.15000	15	COOP	1964	Present	NO
Yakutat	59.51667	-139.66667	9	COOP	1949	Present	NO
Beaver Creek	62.41667	-140.85000	655	NRCS-SC	1975	Present	NO
Chair Mountain	62.06667	-140.80000	1158	NRCS-SC	1988	Present	NO
Chistochina	62.55000	-144.60000	701	NRCS-SC	1985	Present	NO
Haggard Creek	62.70000	-145.45000	732	NRCS-SC	1964	Present	NO
Jatahmund Lake	63.61667	-141.96667	701	NRCS-SC	1993	Present	NO
Kenny Lake	61.73333	-144.98333	396	NRCS-SC	1980	Present	NO
Mentasta Pass	62.90000	-143.66667	741	NRCS-SC	1962	Present	NO
Paradise Hill	62.80000	-141.30000	671	NRCS-SC	1992	Present	NO
Paxson	63.01667	-145.50000	808	NRCS-SC	1982	Present	NO
Tazlina	62.04167	-145.41667	373	NRCS-SC	1996	Present	NO
Tok Junction	63.30000	-143.00000	503	NRCS-SC	1960	Present	NO
Tolsona Creek	62.10000	-146.05000	610	NRCS-SC	1985	Present	NO
Tsaina River	61.20000	-145.50000	503	NRCS-SC	1972	Present	NO
Worthington Glacier	61.18333	-145.68333	640	NRCS-SC	1958	Present	NO
Alcan Hwy Mile 1244	62.81667	-141.46667	579	RAWS	1998	Present	NO
Bering Glacier	60.11861	-143.28333	23	RAWS	1998	Present	NO
Chistochina	62.56528	-144.66472	701	RAWS	2001	Present	NO
Chitina	61.53194	-144.43972	177	RAWS	1998	Present	NO
Jatahmund Lake	62.60000	-142.70389	701	RAWS	1990	Present	NO
Paxson	63.03444	-145.49667	814	RAWS	1996	Present	NO
Tok River Valley	62.95722	-143.34667	701	RAWS	1999	Present	NO
Cordova	60.50000	-145.50000	12	SAO	1949	Present	NO
Gulkana	62.15000	-145.45000	479	SAO	1949	Present	NO
Northway	62.96667	-141.93333	521	SAO	1949	Present	NO
Yakutat	59.51028	-139.62778	9	SAO	1936	Present	NO
Northway	62.97000	-141.97000	524	Upper Air	1942	1955	NO
Yakutat	59.50000	-139.67000	9	Upper Air	1944	Present	NO
Yukon-Charley Rivers National Preserve (YUCH)							
Cathedral Mountain	65.17407	-143.14387	549	NRCS-AM	2002	Present	YES
Copper Creek	64.86852	-143.39677	610	NRCS-AM	2002	Present	YES
Crescent Creek	64.85280	-143.94443	792	NRCS-AM	2003	Present	YES
Tacoma	65.43987	-143.74587	442	NRCS-AM	2002	Present	YES
Three Fingers	65.64844	-143.15283	1021	NRCS-AM	2002	Present	YES
Coal Creek	65.31667	-143.16667	305	NRCS-SC	2002	Present	YES
Ben Creek	65.28333	-143.06666	564	RAWS	1990	Present	YES

Name	Lat.	Lon.	Elev. (m)	Network	Start	End	In Park?
Coal Creek	65.30413	-143.15701	292	RAWS	2004	Present	YES
Upper Charley River	64.51692	-143.20238	1114	RAWS	2005	Present	YES
Chicken	64.09167	-141.92111	549	COOP	1996	Present	NO
Eagle	64.76667	-141.20000	247	COOP	1949	Present	NO
Step Mountain	65.44562	-141.34963	869	NRCS-AM	2002	Present	NO
Mission Creek	64.78333	-141.20000	274	NRCS-SC	1989	Present	NO
Birch Creek	65.58472	-144.36361	259	RAWS	1998	Present	NO
Eagle	64.77611	-141.16194	268	RAWS	1992	Present	NO
Eagle	64.77677	-141.14833	274	SAO	1998	Present	NO

5.0 Conclusions and Recommendations

We offer next an evaluation and general comments pertaining to the status, prospects, and needs for climate-monitoring capabilities in CAKN. These include remarks on the overall strategy, differences among park units, and other issues for which there is no obvious choice of logical order. These findings are based on examination of the available records, discussions with NPS staff and other collaborators, and prior knowledge and studies of climate and its topographical variability. Related comments for the CAKN were previously offered by Redmond and Simeral (2004) in evaluating specific potential climate station sites.

5.1 General Comments

CAKN has previously assessed the state of observational infrastructure for weather and climate and has begun to act upon those findings. In so doing, over the past several years the NPS I&M staff have assembled an impressive amount of material about practical details and have simultaneously helped develop the philosophical underpinnings for this and other I&M networks. The CAKN climate evaluations and activities have been very thorough. Their logical and methodical approach has been a model that other I&M networks would do well to emulate. Aspects of this task might be easier in Alaska because of the major federal presence and the history of interagency relationships, and because most of the weather and climate data have been gathered under such auspices. The CAKN network has also benefited from having the services of a specialist largely dedicated to this topic.

The first priority is that each of the three main park units have some degree of geographically distributed stations, and that goal is in the process of being realized. Reflecting popularity, visitation, accessibility, historical establishment, and physical diversity among the three park units, DENA appears to have the best temporal and spatial climate station representation, followed by WRST and then YUCH. Although YUCH has the fewest long-term records within park boundaries, it also has the least climatic diversity.

Any existing manual stations should continue in perpetuity. These records are heavily utilized by visitors and researchers alike, and are automatically fed into a comprehensive national system. They are the only long-term measurements available, are the only source of snowfall measurements, and can provide reliable and accurate precipitation measurements throughout winter. Every effort should be made (in concert with NOAA) to insure that these observations make their way promptly into the national archive, and that all gaps in the historical record (likely stemming from delayed submission) are back-filled. WRCC personnel are willing to help with this process.

The CAKN has mapped out an effective strategy (MacCluskie and Oakley 2002, MacCluskie and Oakley 2003; MacCluskie et al. 2004; Sousanes and Adema 2004) for deciding ongoing and future priorities. Geographic coverage, elevation coverage, clustering and transects, and logistical issues have been anticipated, as well as potential partnership and leveraging opportunities. Automated measurements form a significant part of this strategy and need to be employed. A significant obstacle to the deployment of such stations continues to be problems with precipitation measurement in frozen environments, which are still far from being resolved,

Multiple observation methods that back each other up need to be employed to address this issue, including any methods that have shown high reliability in the past. Automation is not a panacea, and does not reduce either the cost of monitoring or the need for human beings, but rather changes what people need to do and the skill sets that are required.

The plan for DENA looks sound and on its way to fulfillment. The addition of SNOTEL-type precipitation gages on the moist south side of the Alaska Range would help fill a geographic gap for that element. A robust, durable, and rugged station at mid-elevation amidst the ice and snow (perhaps without precipitation) would start to address the low-elevation bias in the planned monitoring program.

Likewise, the strategy for WRST also looks sound. Major ice masses are perched near the mean annual freezing isotherm, especially on the ocean side. One or two high capacity precipitation gages (with other instrumentation) close to their southern flanks would help fill a gap. The notion of employing north-south transects across the maritime to continental transition has great merit. The difficulty of finding even one climate station with just a moderately-long-term, homogeneous, complete, and reliable record within this vast tract of land underscores the necessity of working toward that goal.

With no long-term records inside or close to the boundary, YUCH poses a more difficult challenge in some ways. The terrain is less forbidding than the other two CAKN units, but the harsh climate is hard on instruments. The reliance on stations outside park boundaries for a long term climate perspective emphasizes the need to work with individuals and agencies who are engaged in such efforts. The proposed set of upland and lowland measurement sites appear reasonable.

In all three park units, climate is often sharply stratified by elevation, and over very short horizontal distances. Any approach that utilizes stations closely spaced horizontally but well separated in elevation is likely to produce very useful knowledge, especially if full (expensive) stations are supplemented by less expensive sensors at intermediate levels. The very lack of long-term, spatially dense measurements of temperature (and precipitation) has hampered development of climate mapping techniques such as PRISM.

A thorough assessment of the spatial representativeness of climate measurements in the CAKN would require knowledge of the temporal and spatial correlation field of each of the different climate elements across a variety of time scales and for the different seasons. Such a correlation analysis is beyond the scope of this report, but a similar analysis was performed by Redmond et al. (2005) for the nearby SWAN network, and many of the conclusions from that study are pertinent to the CAKN area.

Based on the SWAN correlation analysis, we expect that in CAKN temperature has much larger scale correlation structure than does precipitation, and that temperatures are spatially better correlated (higher r values over larger areas (at a given elevation)) than are precipitation totals. This can be taken as a measure of the role of the Aleutian Low and how pervasively it controls the large scale flow into southern Alaska. Figures showing the annual cycle of large scale wind patterns at the surface and at about 3000 m (pressure level 700 mb) over Alaska and the adjoining North Pacific can be found in Figures 22-24 in Redmond et al. (2005).

During the winter months, when the Aleutian Low exerts its greatest influence, pairwise correlations of mean monthly temperature computed for the adjoining southwest park units (Redmond et al. 2005) in the SWAN area were generally found to be around r = 0.90. These very high values arise largely because the main flow is southerly, from the ocean toward land. In summer, temperature correlations are generally lower, for two reasons. One is that local effects are more influential. The second is that the variances are quite low; at a given location there is not as much variation from year to year between various Julys or Augusts, for example, as there is between year-to-year Januarys or Februarys, so that small absolute anomaly differences can readily lower correlations. Maximum and minimum temperatures usually show different behavior from each other, depending on season and on elevation difference. In general maximum temperatures correlate better with each other than do minimum temperatures, since maximum temperatures are more frequently controlled by larger scale factors, and have better ties to the overlying ("free") atmosphere. Minimum temperatures are typically much more subject to local influences. The best minimum temperature correlations are usually found between adjoining ridges, rather than mid-slopes or valleys. Of the three CAKN units, the SWAN correlations of temperature are most applicable to WRST.

Deeper in the interior portions of Alaska, inversions are very common during winter except during windy periods, so that the coldest air is usually found in the lowest elevations. Inversions can be very intense, with variations of 10-30°C quite common in the lowest couple hundred meters. Thus, a mix of stations at different elevations is needed to adequately sample this variation (for example, at least one bottom station and one ridge top station included to bracket the range). Inversion frequency and strength varies naturally and may show systematic climate change effects, so temporal trends ("climate change") need not be the same at different elevations.

For precipitation, spatial correlations from the SWAN area were generally lower, sometimes much lower, than for temperature. Taking into account possible problems with winter precipitation data quality, we conclude that our uncertainties about spatial patterns of temporal precipitation variability are greater than those for temperature, with a greater need for quality precipitation measurements. However, we also recognize that good measurements of precipitation are much harder to obtain for the long periods (usually 10-20 years or more) needed for adequate correlation analysis.

5.2 Spatial Variations in Mean Climate

Topography is a major controlling factor on the park units within CAKN, leading to systematic spatial variations in mean surface climate. With local variations over short horizontal and vertical distances, topography introduces considerable fine-scale structure to mean climate (temperature and precipitation). Issues encountered in mapping mean climate are discussed in Appendix E and in Redmond et al. (2005).

If only a few stations will be emplaced, the primary goal should be overall characterization of the main climate elements (temperature and precipitation, and snow). This level of characterization generally requires that (a) stations should not be located in deep valley bottoms (cold air drainage pockets) or near excessively steep slopes and (b) stations should be distributed spatially in the major biomes of each park. If such stations already are present in the vicinity, then additional stations would be best used for two important and somewhat competing purposes: (a) add redundancy as backup for loss of data from current stations (or loss of the physical stations) or (b) provide added information on spatial heterogeneity in climate arising from topographic diversity, particularly inversions.

The desirability of credible and accurate long-term complete climate records, from any location, cannot be overstressed. This consideration should thus always have a high priority. However, because of spatial and elevation diversity in climate, monitoring that fills knowledge gaps, and in the bargain provides information on long-term temporal variability in short-distance relationships, will also likely prove of inestimable value. We cannot be sure that climate variability and climate change will affect all parts of a given park unit equally; it is in fact a safe bet that this is not the case, and that the spatial variations in temporal variability extend to small spatial scales (a few km or less in some cases), a consequence of extreme elevation diversity.

5.3 Climate Change Detection

The high latitudes are likely to be some of the first regions to experience the effects of climate change, most obviously through effects of temperature on boreal ecosystems (including release of carbon and methane), large masses of ice near critical temperatures, significant areas of permafrost now just below freezing, and behavior of fish and wildlife (Hinzman et al. 2005; Arctic Climate Impact Assessment 2004). Though there is not as much agreement about potential precipitation changes as about temperature changes, there is a general consensus among models that higher latitudes will probably become wetter. Alaska parks are therefore in a unique position, and adequate monitoring of all potentially affected systems should be well under way before any such changes become widespread.

Parts of the Alaska Range and of the Chugach Range are near the mean annual freezing mark. In these zones, small changes that move temperature from below to above freezing have significant potential to affect mass balance of icefields, and to affect the character of storms by increasing the ratio of rain to snow. The elevation of the rain/snow line, the manner of accumulation during the winter, the way the snowpack ripens in the spring, the timing of the spring snowmelt runoff pulse, and the summer loss of ice, would all be affected by changes in temperature. At lower elevations, permafrost changes are a major concern, from ecological and practical standpoints. Indeed, changes in permafrost (e.g., Jorgenson et al. 2001; Hinzman et al. 2005) and in beginning date of spring snowmelt (Stewart et al. 2004) have already been noted in Alaska. Other thresholds may be of significance, such as locations whose warmest mean monthly or mean monthly maximum temperature is near freezing (generally high elevations) or whose coolest mean monthly or monthly minimum is not far from freezing (southern coasts).

For these reasons, those sites that have mean annual temperatures just below freezing (approximately 1-3°C below freezing) would constitute particularly attractive candidate locations to monitor climate changes. Such locations might be expected to show new behavior if a biological temperature control (either warm or cool, or lack of warmth or lack of cool) is either removed or caused to be much less likely. Certain insect pests that affect trees are held in check by the occurrence of very cold temperatures each winter. See for example the model of Thomson, Perkins, Safranyik and Benton found at

47

http://www.pfc.forestry.ca/climate/change/beetle_e.html and based on the paper of Safranyik et al. (1975). The lack of such temperatures, or a decrease in their frequency, could release an important environmental control and lead to infestation. As in other locations, it is quite likely that the ranges of a number of plant and animal species are controlled by (species-specific) particular threshold temperatures. Thus, in anticipation of any of these changing, a broad sampling of climate regimes constitutes the best initial strategy.

It is not certain that these effects would be the same at all elevations. The Pacific Ocean is a tremendous flywheel for stored energy, and changes in temperature next to the ocean may differ from changes in the interior across the Alaska Range.

Based on climate change considerations alone, a recommended strategy would entail station placement in the pure coastal zone, in the pure interior zone, at higher elevations closer to the location of what is now quasi-permanent ice, and in transition regions such as drainage divides. The idea of transects spanning transitions from marine to interior climates has great merit.

5.4 Aesthetics

This issue arises frequently enough to deserve comment. Standards for quality climate measurements require open exposures away from heat sources, buildings, pavement, close vegetation and tall trees, and human intrusion (thus away from property lines). By their nature, sites that meet these standards are usually quite visible. In many settings (such as heavily forested areas) these sites also are quite rare, making them precisely the same places that managers wish to protect from aesthetic intrusion. The most suitable and scientifically defensible sites frequently are rejected as candidate locations for weather/climate stations. Most weather/climate stations, therefore, tend to be "hidden" but many of these hidden locations have inferior exposures. Some measure of compromise is nearly always called for in siting weather and climate stations.

The public has vast interest and curiosity in weather and climate, and within the NPS I&M networks, such measurements consistently rate near or at the top of desired public information. There seem to be many possible opportunities for exploiting and embracing this widespread interest within the interpretive mission of the NPS. One way to do this would be to highlight rather than hide certain stations and educate the public about the need for adequate siting. A number of weather displays we have encountered during visits have proven inadvertently to serve as counterexamples for how measurements should *not* be made. Camouflage techniques can also be quite effective in making stations less obvious (although a few principles cannot be compromised, such as white housings for thermometers, and good exposure for wind).

5.5 Additional Factors

Appendix E discusses a number of factors that should be considered in making decisions about monitoring strategies. All are important, but just a few will be highlighted as they pertain to the CAKN.

The types of climates in central and coastal Alaska are notoriously unkind to instrumentation. Cold is more tolerable (for instruments) than is precipitation, and liquid precipitation is much more instrument-friendly than frozen precipitation. The lack of AC power precludes heating for precipitation and anemometers. In this harsh region, without experienced and skilled technical personnel to oversee stations and communications, the odds of failure (missing, intermittent, or low quality data) are high. The cautions in Appendix E are even more applicable here than in the contiguous 48 states. Sites are remote, communications are difficult to maintain, human access is expensive and often affected by weather events, and visits to sites can seldom be impromptu. Animals of all sizes and inclinations can interact with stations in myriad ways. Sites can be buried in snow, automated equipment and electronics can be subjected to severe conditions at or beyond design criteria for wind, cold, snow, or precipitation. Station communications are often only one-way, preventing reprogramming or backfilling interrupted transmissions. In the end, it is almost always logistics, maintenance and other practical factors that determine the success of weather and climate monitoring activities.

At these latitudes the term "higher elevations" could be approximately taken to be elevations between 900-1800 m or higher. This is about the level where the tops of some of the main ice fields are found. Stations at the highest elevations (above 4500 m) are a laudable goal, and have both climatic and safety benefits, but require dedicated individuals and almost always heroic effort to maintain.

For this particular region, the need for care expressed in the Appendix E for individual climate elements are particularly germane for the measurement of precipitation, a large fraction of which is snow. Gages that measure frozen precipitation accurately (to within 0.25 mm) are expensive, but a few should be considered. Generally these operate on a weighing principle; such gages do need to be watched by real human beings, emptied and recharged with antifreeze periodically. Experience from the Sierra Nevada shows such automated gages might need to be emptied in parts of WRST every few weeks, or even days in some cases, during the heavy precipitation season. Less accurate gages like those used by SNOTEL do not record smaller events very well, but do give accurate aggregate seasonal totals, and often need no tending all winter.

At these higher latitudes, the sun can be found at low angles in summer in the northern part of the sky, so a good portion of the southern horizon needs to be free of terrain and vegetation blockage than in lower latitudes. For example, on June 21 (2004 for example), in Anchorage (61 N latitude) the sun rises just 33 degrees east of north, and crosses the eastern azimuth at a height of 27 degrees, reaches a maximum elevation angle of 52 degrees above the southern horizon, crosses west at 27 degrees and drops below the horizon 33 degrees west of north. Six months later, the sun rises 55 degrees south of east, crosses the meridian only 6 degrees above the horizon, and sets 55 degrees south of west. Only a pyranometer in a fairly flat location without nearby mountain peaks will record the direct beam contribution every day of the year. In most locations, trees or mountains will block part of the day. Solar panels often fail to provide sufficient battery recharge, especially when cloudy, and especially when covered with snow.

Soil temperature is relatively inexpensive to measure, and should be measured at a few stations. Climate variability is large in this area, and slow changes in temperature from climate change would change many aspects of biological activity in the soil as well as extend the biologically active time of the year. In areas with permafrost, the value of soil temperature monitoring is greater yet.

In WRST and DENA, local climate changes could be accentuated in the vicinity of receding glacial features. Local conditions may become more "balmy" and change rapidly as the ice withdraws, even if the ice is responding to regional climate over the last decade or two. In this case, a lightly vegetated prominence away from the direct influence of the ice (as thru reflected solar radiation, or glacially induced winds), and at about the middle elevation of the ice, would be a more appropriate location for a station.

The park units of the CAKN are very large (DENA: 2.5 million hectares, WRST: 5.3 million hectares, YUCH: 1 million hectares; for comparison, Yellowstone National Park encompasses 900,000 hectares) and have a considerable degree of variability within each one. Considering the climatic diversity present in these park units, it is impossible to represent such large areas with single stations. Of the three park units in the CAKN, YUCH is the least inhomogeneous, and WRST has the greatest internal diversity of climate within the outer boundaries.

At a minimum, each park unit should have at least 3-5 observing sites within its boundaries, and DENA and WRST are at or close to that number. The entire area has sparse data, and the coastal and ice/snow zones are the most undersampled areas. There should be at least two higher elevation sites in those park units that contain high-elevation zones. There is one very high site on Denali, deployed by mountaineers. This site has been very difficult to keep running, however, due to the extremely demanding conditions that are present on this mountain.

5.6 Information Access

Access to information promotes its use, which in turn promotes attention to station care and maintenance, better data, and more use. An end-to-end view that extends from sensing to decision support is far preferable to isolated and disconnected activities and aids the support infrastructure that is ultimately so necessary for successful, long-term climate monitoring.

Decisions about improvements in monitoring capacity are facilitated greatly by the ability to examine available climate information. Various methods are being created at WRCC to improve access to that information. Web pages providing historic and ongoing climate data, and information from CAKN park units can be accessed at www.wrcc.dri.edu/nps. In the event that this URL changes, there still will be links from the main WRCC Web page entitled "Projects" under NPS.

The WRCC has been steadily developing software to summarize data from hourly sites. This has been occurring under the aegis of the RAWS program and a growing array of product generators ranging from daily and monthly data lists to wind roses and hourly frequency distributions. All park data are available to park personnel via an access code (needed only for data listings) that can be acquired by request. The WRCC RAWS Web page is located at www.raws.dri.edu.

Web pages have been developed to provide access not only to historic and ongoing climate data and information from CAKN park units but also to climate-monitoring efforts for CAKN. These pages can be found through www.wrcc.dri.edu/nps.

Additional access to more standard climate information is accessible though the previously mentioned Web pages, as well as through www.wrcc.dri.edu/summary. These summaries are generally for COOP stations.

5.7 Summarized Conclusions and Recommendations

- Excellent cooperation and assistance from CAKN personnel – very high-quality effort and a good model for other networks.
- Comprehensive background material, providing a sound basis for planning.
- Many environmental and physical factors vulnerable to climate warming.
- Region poised to experience climate change, needs careful recording.
- Main deficiencies previously identified; most are being addressed.
- Long-term records inside WRST and YUCH not as good as inside DENA.
- Reliable measurement of frozen precipitation at relatively few sites.
- Retain key long-term manual stations, avoid further moves or gaps.
- Severe conditions - need dependable technology with known track record.
- Significant human and technical resources required for continued success.
- Integrate climate as interpretive strength of these park units.
- Alpine elevations under-represented if climate change varies with altitude.

6.0 Literature Cited

American Association of State Climatologists. 1985. Heights and Exposure Standards for Sensors on Automated Weather Stations. The State Climatologist **9**(4).

Arctic Climate Impact Assessment. 2004. Available from http://www.acia.uaf.edu (accessed 26 November 2004).

Blauveldt, K. 2005. High Plains Climate Center Maintenance and Calibration Manual for the Automated Weather Data Network. Calibration Facility, Automated Weather Data Network, High Plains Climate Center, University of Nebraska, Lincoln, NE. Available from http://www.atmos.washington.edu/~mantua/REPORTS/PDO/PDO_cs.htm (accessed 19 March 2005).

Bering Sea Impacts Study (BESIS). 1997. The impacts of global climate change in the Bering Sea region. An assessment conducted by the International Arctic Science Committee under its Bering Sea Impacts Study (BESIS), International Arctic Science Committee, Oslo Norway. Available from http://www.besis.uaf.edu (accessed 1 June 2005).

Bonan, G. B. 2002. Ecological Climatology: Concepts and Applications. Cambridge University Press.

Bureau of Land Management. 1997. Remote Automatic Weather Station (RAWS) and Remote Environmental Monitoring Systems (REMS) Standards. RAWS/REMS Support Facility, Boise, Idaho.

CAKN. 2004. Central Alaska Network Geologic Resources Evaluation Scoping Meeting Summary. Central Alaska Inventory and Monitoring Network, Anchorage, AK. Available at http://www2.nature.nps.gov/geology/inventory/publications/s_summaries/CAKN_GRE_Scoping_Summary_View.pdf (accessed 23 April 2006).

Chapin, F. S. III, M. S. Torn, and M. Tateno. 1996. Principles of ecosystem sustainability. American Naturalist **148**(6):1016-1037.

Daly, C., R. P. Neilson, and D. L. Phillips. 1994. A Statistical-Topographic Model for Mapping Climatological Precipitation over Mountainous Terrain. Journal of Applied Meteorology **33**:140-158.

Daly, C., W. P. Gibson, G. H. Taylor, G. L. Johnson, and P. Pasteris. 2002. A knowledge-based approach to the statistical mapping of climate. Climate Research **22**:99-113.

Doggett, M., C. Daly, J. Smith, W. Gibson, G. Taylor, G. Johnson, and P. Pasteris. 2004. High-resolution 1971-2000 mean monthly temperature maps for the western United States. Fourteenth AMS Conf. on Applied Climatology, 84th AMS Annual Meeting. Seattle, WA, American Meteorological Society, Boston, MA, January 2004, Paper 4.3, CD-ROM.

Environmental Protection Agency. 1987. On-Site Meteorological Program Guidance for Regulatory Modeling Applications. EPA-450/4-87-013. Environmental Protection Agency, Office of Air Quality Planning and Standards, Research Triangle Park, NC.

Finklin, A. I., and W. C. Fischer. 1990. Weather Station Handbook –an Interagency Guide for Wildland Managers. NFES No. 2140. National Wildfire Coordinating Group, Boise, Idaho.

Gibson, W. P., C. Daly, T. Kittel, D. Nychka, C. Johns, N. Rosenbloom, A. McNab, and G. Taylor. 2002. Development of a 103-year high-resolution climate data set for the conterminous United States. Thirteenth AMS Conf. on Applied Climatology. Portland, OR, American Meteorological Society, Boston, MA, May 2002:181-183.

Hinzman, L. D., N. D. Bettez, W. R. Bolton, F. S. Chapin, M. B. Dyurgerov, C. L. Fastie, B. Griffith, R. D. Hollister, A. Hope, H. P. Huntington, and others. 2005. Evidence and implications of recent climate change in northern Alaska and other Arctic regions. Climatic Change **72**(3):251-298.

I&M. 2006. I&M Inventories home page. http://science.nature.nps.gov/im/inventory/index.cfm.

Jacobson, M. C., R. J. Charlson, H. Rodhe, and G. H. Orians. 2000. Earth System Science: From Biogeochemical Cycles to Global Change. Academic Press, San Diego.

Jorgenson, M. T., C. H. Racine, J. C. Walters and T. E. Osterkamp. 2001. Permafrost degradation and ecological changes associeated with a warming climate in central Alaska. Climatic Change **48**(4):551-579.

Karl, T. R., V. E. Derr, D. R. Easterling, C. K. Folland, D. J. Hoffman, S. Levitus, N. Nicholls, D. E. Parker, and G. W. Withee. 1996. Critical Issues for Long-Term Climate Monitoring. Pages 55-92 *in* T. R. Karl, editor. Long Term Climate Monitoring by the Global Climate Observing System, Kluwer Publishing.

Kunkel, K. E., K. G. Hubbard, D. Easterling, D. Robinson, and K. T. Redmond. 2006. Issues with identification of trends in 20th Century U.S. snowfall. Journal of Atmospheric and Oceanic Technology, submitted.

MacCluskie, M., and K. Oakley. 2002. Central Alaska Network Vital Signs Monitoring Plan. Phase I Report. Available from http://www.nature.nps.gov/im/units/cakn/reportpubs.cfm (accessed 1 March 2006).

MacCluskie, M., and K. Oakley. 2003. Central Alaska Network Vital Signs Monitoring Plan. Phase II Report. Available from http://www.nature.nps.gov/im/units/cakn/reportpubs.cfm (accessed 1 March 2006).

MacCluskie, M., K. Oakley, T. McDonald, and D. Wilder. 2004. Central Alaska Network Vital Signs Monitoring Plan. Phase III Report. Available from http://www.nature.nps.gov/im/units/cakn/reportpubs.cfm (accessed 1 March 2006).

Mantua, N. J., S. R. Hare, Y. Zhang, J. M. Wallace, and R. C. Francis. 1997. A Pacific interdecadal climate oscillation with impacts on salmon production. Bulletin of the American Meteorological Society **78**:1069-1079.

National Research Council. 2001. A Climate Services Vision: First Steps Toward the Future. National Academies Press, Washington, D.C.

National Wildfire Coordinating Group. 2004. National Fire Danger Rating System Weather Station Standards. Report PMS 426.3. National Wildfire Coordinating Group, Boise, Idaho.

Neilson, R. P. 1987. Biotic regionalization and climatic controls in western North America. Vegetatio **70**:135-147.

Oakley, K. L, and S. L. Boudreau. 2000. Conceptual Design of the Long-term Ecological Monitoring Program for Denali National Park and Preserve. Available at www.absc.usgs.gov/research/Denali_USGS/downloads/Denali_LTEM_Report_without_cover.pdf (accessed 1 December 2005).

Oakley, K. L., L. P. Thomas, and S. G. Fancy. 2003. Guidelines for long-term monitoring protocols. Wildlife Society Bulletin **31**:1000-1003.

Redmond, K. T. and D. B. Simeral. 2004. Climate Monitoring Comments: Central Alaska Network Inventory and Monitoring Program. Available from ftp://ftp.wrcc.dri.edu/nps/alaska/cakn/npscakncomments040406.pdf (accessed 6 April 2004).

Redmond, K. T., D. B. Simeral, and G. D. McCurdy. 2005. Climate Monitoring for Southwest Alaska National Parks: Network Design and Site Selection. Report 05-01. Western Regional Climate Center, Reno, Nevada.

Redmond, K. T. 2006. Climate variability and change as a backdrop for western resource management. Conference Proceedings. "Bringing Climate into Natural Resource Management," Portland, OR, USDA Forest Service, Pacific Northwest Research Station, Portland, OR, June 2005.

Safranyik, L., D. M. Shrimpton, and H. S. Whitney. 1975. An interpretation of the interaction between lodgepole pine, the Mountain Pine Beetle and its associated blue stain fungi in Western Canada. Pages 406-428 *in* D.M. Baumgartner, editor. Management of Lodgepole Pine Ecosystems. Washington State University Cooperative Extension Service, Pullman, WA.

Schlesinger, W. H. 1997. Biogeochemistry: An Analysis of Global Change. Academic Press, San Diego.

Sousanes, P. J., and G. Adema. 2004. Climate Monitoring Protocol for the Central Alaska Network Denali National Park and Preserve, Yukon-Charley Rivers National Preserve, and Wrangell-St. Elias National Park and Preserve. General Technical Report. Central Alaska Inventory and Monitoring Network, Anchorage, AK.

Stewart, I. T., D. R. Cayan, and M. D. Dettinger. 2004. Changes in Snowmelt Runoff Timing in Western North America under a 'Business as Usual' Climate Change Scenario. Climatic Change **62**:217-232.

Tanner, B. D. 1990. Automated Weather Stations. Remote Sensing Reviews **5**(1):73-98.

Whitford, W. G. 2002. Ecology of Desert Systems. Academic Press. San Diego.

World Meteorological Organization. 1983. Guide to Meteorological Instruments and Methods of Observation, No. 8, 5th edition, World Meteorological Organization, Geneva Switzerland.

World Meteorological Organization. 2005. Organization and planning of intercomparisons of rainfall intensity gauges. World Meteorological Organization, Geneva Switzerland.

Appendix A. Climate-monitoring principles.

Since the late 1990s, frequent references have been made to a set of climate-monitoring principles enunciated in 1996 by Tom Karl, director of the NOAA NCDC in Asheville, North Carolina. These monitoring principles also have been referred to informally as the "Ten Commandments of Climate Monitoring." Both versions are given here. In addition, these principles have been adopted by the Global Climate Observing System (GCOS 2004).

(Compiled by Kelly Redmond, Western Regional Climate Center, Desert Research Institute, August 2000.)

A.1 Full Version (Karl et al. 1996)

A. Effects on climate records of instrument changes, observing practices, observation locations, sampling rates, etc., must be known before such changes are implemented. This can be ascertained through a period where overlapping measurements from old and new observing systems are collected or sometimes by comparing the old and new observing systems with a reference standard. Site stability for in situ measurements, both in terms of physical location and changes in the nearby environment, also should be a key criterion in site selection. Thus, many synoptic network stations, which are primarily used in weather forecasting but also provide valuable climate data, and dedicated climate stations intended to be operational for extended periods must be subject to this policy.

B. Processing algorithms and changes in these algorithms must be well documented. Documentation should be carried with the data throughout the data-archiving process.

C. Knowledge of instrument, station, and/or platform history is essential for interpreting and using the data. Changes in instrument sampling time, local environmental conditions for in situ measurements, and other factors pertinent to interpreting the observations and measurements should be recorded as a mandatory part in the observing routine and be archived with the original data.

D. In situ and other observations with a long, uninterrupted record should be maintained. Every effort should be applied to protect the data sets that have provided long-term, homogeneous observations. "Long-term" for space-based measurements is measured in decades, but for more conventional measurements, "long-term" may be a century or more. Each element in the observational system should develop a list of prioritized sites or observations based on their contribution to long-term climate monitoring.

E. Calibration, validation, and maintenance facilities are critical requirements for long-term climatic data sets. Homogeneity in the climate record must be assessed routinely, and corrective action must become part of the archived record.

F. Where feasible, some level of "low-technology" backup to "high-technology" observing systems should be developed to safeguard against unexpected operational failures.

G. Regions having insufficient data, variables and regions sensitive to change, and key measurements lacking adequate spatial and temporal resolution should be given the highest priority in designing and implementing new climate-observing systems.

H. Network designers and instrument engineers must receive long-term climate requirements at the outset of the network design process. This is particularly important because most observing systems have been designed for purposes other than long-term climate monitoring. Instruments must possess adequate accuracy with biases small enough to document climate variations and changes.

I. Much of the development of new observational capabilities and the evidence supporting the value of these observations stem from research-oriented needs or programs. A lack of stable, long-term commitment to these observations and lack of a clear transition plan from research to operations are two frequent limitations in the development of adequate, long-term monitoring capabilities. Difficulties in securing a long-term commitment must be overcome in order to improve the climate-observing system in a timely manner with minimal interruptions.

J. Data management systems that facilitate access, use, and interpretation are essential. Freedom of access, low cost, mechanisms that facilitate use (directories, catalogs, browse capabilities, availability of metadata on station histories, algorithm accessibility and documentation, etc.) and quality control should guide data management. International cooperation is critical for successful management of data used to monitor long-term climate change and variability.

A.2 Abbreviated version, "Ten Commandments of Climate Monitoring"

A. Assess the impact of new climate-observing systems or changes to existing systems before they are implemented.

"Thou shalt properly manage network change." (assess effects of proposed changes)

B. Require a suitable period where measurement from new and old climate-observing systems will overlap.

"Thou shalt conduct parallel testing." (compare old and replacement systems)

C. Treat calibration, validation, algorithm-change, and data-homogeneity assessments with the same care as the data.

"Thou shalt collect metadata." (fully document system and operating procedures)

D. Verify capability for routinely assessing the quality and homogeneity of the data including high-resolution data for extreme events.

"Thou shalt assure data quality and continuity." (assess as part of routine operating procedures)

E. Integrate assessments like those conducted by the International Panel on Climate Change into global climate-observing priorities.

"Thou shalt anticipate the use of data." (integrated environmental assessment; component in operational plan for system)

F. Maintain long-term weather and climate stations.

"Thou shalt worship historic significance." (maintain homogeneous data sets from long–term, climate-observing systems)

G. Place high priority on increasing observations in regions lacking sufficient data and in regions sensitive to change and variability.

"Thou shalt acquire complementary data." (new sites to fill observational gaps)

H. Provide network operators, designers, and instrument engineers with long-term requirements at the outset of the design and implementation phases for new systems.

"Thou shalt specify requirements for climate observation systems." (application and usage of observational data)

I. Carefully consider the transition from research-observing system to long-term operation.

"Thou shalt have continuity of purpose." (stable long-term commitments)

J. Focus on data-management systems that facilitate access, use, and interpretation of weather data and metadata.

"Thou shalt provide access to data and metadata." (readily-available weather and climate information)

A.3 Literature Cited

Karl, T. R., V. E. Derr, D. R. Easterling, C. K. Folland, D. J. Hoffman, S. Levitus, N. Nicholls, D. E. Parker, and G. W. Withee. 1996. Critical Issues for Long-Term Climate Monitoring. Pages 55-92 *in* T. R. Karl, editor. Long Term Climate Monitoring by the Global Climate Observing System, Kluwer Publishing.

Global Climate Observing System. 2004. Implementation Plan for the Global Observing System for Climate in Support of the UNFCCC. GCOS-92, WMO/TD No. 1219, World Meteorological Organization, Geneva, Switzerland.

Appendix B. Glossary.

Climate—Complete and entire ensemble of statistical descriptors of temporal and spatial properties comprising the behavior of the atmosphere. These descriptors include means, variances, frequency distributions, autocorrelations, spatial correlations and other patterns of association, temporal lags, and element-to-element relationships. The descriptors have a physical basis in flows and reservoirs of energy and mass. Climate and weather phenomena shade gradually into each other and are ultimately inseparable.

Climate Element—(same as Weather Element) Attribute or property of the state of the atmosphere that is measured, estimated, or derived. Examples of climate elements include temperature, wind speed, wind direction, precipitation amount, precipitation type, relative humidity, dewpoint, solar radiation, snow depth, soil temperature at a given depth, etc. A derived element is a function of other elements (like degree days or number of days with rain) and is not measured directly with a sensor. The terms "parameter" or "variable" are not used to describe elements.

Climate Network—Group of climate stations having a common purpose; the group is often owned and maintained by a single organization.

Climate Station—Station where data are collected to track atmospheric conditions over the long-term. Often, this station operates to additional standards to verify long-term consistency. For these stations, the detailed circumstances surrounding a set of measurements (siting and exposure, instrument changes, etc.) are important.

Data—Measurements specifying the state of the physical environment. Does not include metadata.

Data Inventory—Information about overall data properties for each station within a weather or climate network. A data inventory may include start/stop dates, percentages of available data, breakdowns by climate element, counts of actual data values, counts or fractions of data types, etc. These properties must be determined by actually reading the data and thus require the data to be available, accessible, and in a readable format.

NPS I&M Network—A set of NPS park units grouped by a common theme, typically by natural resource and/or geographic region.

Metadata—Information necessary to interpret environmental data properly, organized as a history or series of snapshots—data about data. Examples include details of measurement processes, station circumstances and exposures, assumptions about the site, network purpose and background, types of observations and sensors, pre-treatment of data, access information, maintenance history and protocols, observational methods, archive locations, owner, and station start/end period.

Quality Assurance—Planned and systematic set of activities to provide adequate confidence that products and services are resulting in credible and correct information. Includes quality control.

Quality Control—Evaluation, assessment, and improvement of imperfect data by utilizing other imperfect data.

Station Inventory—Information about a set of stations obtained from metadata that accompany the network or networks. A station inventory can be compiled from direct and indirect reports prepared by others.

Weather—Instantaneous state of the atmosphere at any given time, mainly with respect to its effects on biological activities. As distinguished from climate, weather consists of the short-term (minutes to days) variations in the atmosphere. Popularly, weather is thought of in terms of temperature, precipitation, humidity, wind, sky condition, visibility, and cloud conditions.

Weather Element (same as Climate Element)—Attribute or property of the state of the atmosphere that is measured, estimated, or derived. Examples of weather elements include temperature, wind speed, wind direction, precipitation amount, precipitation type, relative humidity, dewpoint, solar radiation, snow depth, soil temperature at a given depth, etc. A derived weather element is a function of other elements (like degree days or number of days with rain) and is not measured directly. The terms "parameter" and "variable" are not used to describe weather elements.

Weather Network—Group of weather stations usually owned and maintained by a particular organization and usually for a specific purpose.

Weather Station—Station where collected data are intended for near-real-time use with less need for reference to long-term conditions. In many cases, the detailed circumstances of a set of measurements (siting and exposure, instrument changes, etc.) from weather stations are not as important as for climate stations.

Appendix C. Factors in operating a climate network.

C.1 Climate versus Weather
- Climate measurements require *consistency through time.*

C.2 Network Purpose
- Anticipated or desired lifetime.
- Breadth of network mission (commitment by needed constituency).
- Dedicated constituency—no network survives without a dedicated constituency.

C.3 Site Identification and Selection
- Spanning gradients in climate or biomes with transects.
- Issues regarding representative spatial scale—site uniformity versus site clustering.
- Alignment with and contribution to network mission.
- Exposure—ability to measure representative quantities.
- Logistics—ability to service station (Always or only in favorable weather?).
- Site redundancy (positive for quality control, negative for extra resources).
- Power—is AC needed?
- Site security—is protection from vandalism needed?
- Permitting often a major impediment and usually underestimated.

C.4 Station Hardware
- Survival—weather is the main cause of lost weather/climate data.
- Robustness of sensors—ability to measure and record in any condition.
- Quality—distrusted records are worthless and a waste of time and money.
  - High quality—will cost up front but pays off later.
  - Low quality—may provide a lower start-up cost but will cost more later (low cost can be expensive).
- Redundancy—backup if sensors malfunction.
- Ice and snow—measurements are much more difficult than rain measurements.
- Severe environments (expense is about two–three times greater than for stations in more benign settings).

C.5 Communications
- Reliability—live data have a much larger constituency.
- One-way or two-way.
  - Retrieval of missed transmissions.
  - Ability to reprogram data logger remotely.
  - Remote troubleshooting abilities.
  - Continuing versus one-time costs.
- Back-up procedures to prevent data loss during communication outages.
- Live communications increase problems but also increase value.

C.6 Maintenance
- Main reason why networks fail (and most networks do eventually fail!).

- <u>Key</u> issue with nearly every network.
- Who will perform maintenance?
- Degree of commitment and motivation to contribute.
- Periodic? On-demand as needed? Preventive?
- Equipment change-out schedules and upgrades for sensors and software.
- Automated stations require <u>skilled</u> and <u>experienced</u> labor.
- Calibration—sensors often drift (climate).
- Site maintenance essential (constant vegetation, surface conditions, nearby influences).
- Typical automated station will cost about $2K per year to maintain.
- Documentation—photos, notes, visits, changes, essential for posterity.
- Planning for equipment life cycle and technological advances.

C.7 Maintaining Programmatic Continuity and Corporate Knowledge
- Long-term vision and commitment needed.
- Institutionalizing versus personalizing—developing appropriate dependencies.

C.8 Data Flow
- Centralized ingest?
- Centralized access to data and data products?
- Local version available?
- Contract out work or do it yourself?
- Quality control of data.
- Archival.
- Metadata—historic information, not a snapshot. Every station should collect metadata.
- Post-collection processing, multiple data-ingestion paths.

C.9 Products
- Most basic product consists of the data values.
- Summaries.
- Write own applications or leverage existing mechanisms?

C.10 Funding
- Prototype approaches as proof of concept.
- Linking and leveraging essential.
- Constituencies—every network <u>needs</u> a constituency.
- Bridging to practical and operational communities? Live data needed.
- Bridging to counterpart research efforts and initiatives—funding source.
- Creativity, resourcefulness, and persistence usually are essential to success.

C.11 Final Comments
- Deployment is by far the easiest part in operating a network.
- Maintenance is the main issue.
- Best analogy: Operating a network is like raising a child; it requires constant attention.

Source: Western Regional Climate Center (WRCC)

Appendix D. Master metadata field list.

Field Name	Field Type	Field Description
begin_date	date	Effective beginning date for a record.
begin_date_flag	char(2)	Flag describing the known accuracy of the begin date for a station.
best_elevation	float(4)	Best known elevation for a station (in feet).
clim_div_code	char(2)	Foreign key defining climate division code (primary in table: clim_div).
clim_div_key	int2	Foreign key defining climate division for a station (primary in table: clim_div.
clim_div_name	varchar(30)	English name for a climate division.
controller_info	varchar(50)	Person or organization who maintains the identifier system for a given weather or climate network.
country_key	int2	Foreign key defining country where a station resides (primary in table: none).
county_key	int2	Foreign key defining county where a station resides (primary in table: county).
county_name	varchar(31)	English name for a county.
description	text	Any description pertaining to the particular table.
end_date	date	Last effective date for a record.
end_date_flag	char(2)	Flag describing the known accuracy of station end date.
fips_country_code	char(2)	FIPS (federal information processing standards) country code.
fips_state_abbr	char(2)	FIPS state abbreviation for a station.
fips_state_code	char(2)	FIPS state code for a station.
history_flag	char(2)	Describes temporal significance of an individual record among others from the same station.
Id_type_key	int2	Foreign key defining the id_type for a station (usually defined in code).
last_updated	date	Date of last update for a record.
latitude	float(8)	Latitude value.
longitude	float(8)	Longitude value.
name_type_key	int2	"3": COOP station name, "2": best station name.
name	varchar(30)	Station name as known at date of last update entry.
ncdc_state_code	char(2)	NCDC, two-character code identifying U.S. state.
network_code	char(8)	Eight-character abbreviation code identifying a network.
network_key	int2	Foreign key defining the network for a station (primary in table: network).
network_station_id	int4	Identifier for a station in the associated network, which is defined by id_type_key.
remark	varchar(254)	Additional information for a record.
src_quality_code	char(2)	Code describing the data quality for the data source.
state_key	int2	Foreign key defining the U.S. state where a station resides (primary in table: state).
state_name	varchar(30)	English name for a state.
station_alt_name	varchar(30)	Other English names for a station.
station_best_name	varchar(30)	Best, most well-known English name for a station.
time_zone	float4	Time zone where a station resides.
ucan_station_id	int4	Unique station identifier for every station in ACIS.
unit_key	int2	Integer value representing a unit of measure.
updated_by	char(8)	Person who last updated a record.

Field Name	Field Type	Field Description
var_major_id	int2	Defines major climate variable.
var_minor_id	int2	Defines data source within a var_major_id.
zipcode	char(5)	Zipcode where a latitude/longitude point resides.
nps_netcode	char(4)	Network four-character identifier.
nps_netname	varchar(128)	Displayed English name for a network.
parkcode	char(4)	Park four-character identifier.
parkname	varchar(128)	Displayed English name for a park/
Im_network	char(4)	NPS I&M network where park belongs (a net code)/
station_id	varchar(16)	Station identifier.
station_id_type	varchar(16)	Type of station identifier.
network.subnetwork.id	varchar(16)	Identifier of a sub-network in associated network.
subnetwork_key	int2	Foreign key defining sub-network for a station.
subnetwork_name	varchar(30)	English name for a sub-network.
slope	integer	Terrain slope at the location.
aspect	integer	Terrain aspect at the station.
gps	char(1)	Indicator of latitude/longitude recorded via GPS (global positioning system).
site_description	text(0)	Physical description of site.
route_directions	text(0)	Driving route or site access directions.
station_photo_id	integer	Unique identifier associating a group of photos to a station. Group of photos all taken on same date.
photo_id	char(30)	Unique identifier for a photo.
photo_date	datetime	Date photograph taken.
photographer	varchar(64)	Name of photographer.
maintenance_date	datetime	Date of station maintenance visit.
contact_key	Integer	Unique identifier associating contact information to a station.
full_name	varchar(64)	Full name of contact person.
organization	varchar(64)	Organization of contact person.
contact_type	varchar(32)	Type of contact person (operator, administrator, etc.)
position_title	varchar(32)	Title of contact person.
address	varchar(32)	Address for contact person.
city	varchar(32)	City for contact person.
state	varchar(2)	State for contact person.
zip_code	char(10)	Zipcode for contact person.
country	varchar(32)	Country for contact person.
email	varchar(64)	E-mail for contact person.
work_phone	varchar(16)	Work phone for contact person.
contact_notes	text(254)	Other details regarding contact person.
equipment_type	char(30)	Sensor measurement type; i.e., wind speed, air temperature, etc.
Eq_manufacturer	char(30)	Manufacturer of equipment.
Eq_model	char(20)	Model number of equipment.
serial_num	char(20)	Serial number of equipment.
Eq_description	varchar(254)	Description of equipment.
install_date	datetime	Installation date of equipment.
remove_date	datetime	Removal date of equipment.
ref_height	integer	Sensor displacement height from surface.
sampling_interval	varchar(10)	Frequency of sensor measurement.

Appendix E. General design considerations for weather/ climate-monitoring programs.

The process for designing a climate-monitoring program benefits from anticipating design and protocol issues discussed here. Much of this material is been excerpted from a report addressing the Channel Islands National Park (Redmond and McCurdy 2005), where an example is found illustrating how these factors can be applied to a specific setting. Many national park units possess some climate or meteorology feature that sets them apart from more familiar or "standard" settings.

E.1 Introduction

There are several criteria that must be used in deciding to deploy new stations and where these new stations should be sited.

- Where are existing stations located?
- Where have data been gathered in the past (discontinued locations)?
- Where would a new station fill a knowledge gap about basic, long-term climatic averages for an area of interest?
- Where would a new station fill a knowledge gap about how climate behaves over time?
- As a special case for behavior over time, what locations might be expected to show a more sensitive response to climate change?
- How do answers to the preceding questions depend on the climate element? Are answers the same for precipitation, temperature, wind, snowfall, humidity, etc.?
- What role should manual measurements play? How should manual measurements interface with automated measurements?
- Are there special technical or management issues, either present or anticipated in the next 5–15 years, requiring added climate information?
- What unique information is provided in addition to information from existing sites? "Redundancy is bad."
- What nearby information is available to estimate missing observations because observing systems always experience gaps and lose data? "Redundancy is good."
- How would logistics and maintenance affect these decisions?

In relation to the preceding questions, there are several topics that should be considered. The following topics are not listed in a particular order.

E.1.1 Network Purpose

Humans seem to have an almost reflexive need to measure temperature and precipitation, along with other climate elements. These reasons span a broad range from utilitarian to curiosity-driven. Although there are well-known recurrent patterns of need and data use, new uses are always appearing. The number of uses ranges in the thousands. Attempts have been made to categorize such uses (see NRC, 1998; NRC, 2001). Because climate measurements are accumulated over a long time, they should be treated as multi-purpose and should be undertaken in a manner that serves the widest possible applications. Some applications remain constant, while others rise and fall in importance. An insistent issue today may subside, while the next pressing issue of tomorrow barely may be anticipated. The notion that humans might affect the climate of the entire Earth was nearly unimaginable when the national USDA (later NOAA) cooperative weather network began in the late 1800s. Abundant experience has shown, however, that there always will be a demand for a history record of climate measurements and their properties. Experience also shows that there is an expectation that climate measurements will be taken and made available to the general public.

An exhaustive list of uses for data would fill many pages and still be incomplete. In broad terms, however, there are needs to document environmental conditions that disrupt or otherwise affect park operations (e.g., storms and droughts). Design and construction standards are determined by climatological event frequencies that exceed certain thresholds. Climate is a determinant that sometimes attracts and sometimes discourages visitors. Climate may play a large part in the park experience (e.g., Death Valley and heat are nearly synonymous). Some park units are large enough to encompass spatial or elevation diversity in climate, and the sequence of events can vary considerably inside or close to park boundaries. That is, temporal trends and statistics may not be the same everywhere, and this spatial structure should be sampled. The granularity of this structure depends on the presence of topography or large climate gradients or both, such as that found along the U.S. West Coast in summer with the rapid transition from the marine layer to the hot interior.

Plant and animal communities and entire ecosystems react to every nuance in the physical environment. No aspect of weather and climate goes undetected in the natural world. Wilson (1998) proposed "an informal rule of biological evolution" that applies here: "If an organic sensor can be imagined that is capable of detecting any particular environmental signal, a species exists somewhere that possesses this sensor." Every weather and climate event, whether dull or extraordinary to humans, matters to some organism. Dramatic events and creeping incremental change both have consequences to living systems. Extreme events or disturbances can "reset the clock" or "shake up the system" and lead to reverberations that last for years to centuries or longer. Slow change can carry complex nonlinear systems (e.g., any living assemblage) into states where chaotic transitions and new behavior occur. These changes are seldom predictable, typically are observed after the fact, and understood only in retrospect. Climate changes may not be exciting, but as a well-known atmospheric scientist, Mike Wallace, from the University of Washington once noted, "subtle does not mean unimportant".

Thus, individuals who observe the climate should be able to record observations accurately and depict both rapid and slow changes. In particular, an array of artificial influences easily can confound detection of slow changes. The record as provided can contain both real climate variability (that took place in the atmosphere) and fake climate variability (that arose directly from the way atmospheric changes were observed and recorded). As an example, trees growing near a climate station with an excellent anemometer will make it appear that the wind gradually slowed down over many years. Great care must be taken to protect against sources of fake climate variability on the longer-time scales of years to decades. Processes leading to the observed climate are not stationary; rather these processes draw from probability distributions that vary with time. For this reason, climatic time series do not exhibit statistical stationarity. The implications are manifold. There are no true climatic "normals" to which climate inevitably must return. Rather, there are broad ranges of climatic conditions. Climate does not demonstrate exact repetition but instead continual fluctuation and sometimes approximate repetition. In addition, there is always new behavior waiting to occur. Consequently, the business of climate monitoring is never finished, and there is no point where we can state confidently that "enough" is known.

E.1.2 Robustness

The most frequent cause for loss of weather data is the weather itself, the very thing we wish to record. The design of climate and weather observing programs should consider the meteorological equivalent of "peaking power" employed by utilities. Because environmental disturbances have significant effects on ecologic systems, sensors, data loggers, and communications networks should be able to function during the most severe conditions that realistically can be anticipated over the next 50–100 years. Systems designed in this manner are less likely to fail under more ordinary conditions, as well as more likely to transmit continuous, quality data for both tranquil and active periods.

E.1.3 Weather versus Climate

For "weather" measurements, pertaining to what is approximately happening here and now, small moves and changes in exposure are not as critical. For "climate" measurements, where values from different points in time are compared, siting and exposure are critical factors, and it is vitally important that the observing circumstances remain essentially unchanged over the duration of the station record.

Station moves can affect different elements to differing degrees. Even small moves of several meters, especially vertically, can affect temperature records. Hills and knolls act differently from the bottoms of small swales, pockets, or drainage channels (Geiger et al. 2003; Whiteman 2000). Precipitation is probably less subject to change with moves of 50–100 m than other elements (that is, precipitation has less intrinsic variation in small spaces) except if wind flow over the gauge is affected.

E.1.4 Physical Setting

Siting and exposure, and their continuity and consistency through time, significantly influence the climate records produced by a station. These two terms have overlapping connotations. We use the term "siting" in a more general sense, reserving the term "exposure" generally for the particular circumstances affecting the ability of an instrument to record measurements that are representative of the desired spatial or temporal scale.

E.1.5 Measurement Intervals

Climatic processes occur continuously in time, but our measurement systems usually record in discrete chunks of time: for example, seconds, hours, or days. These measurements often are referred to as "systematic" measurements. Interval averages may hide active or interesting periods of highly intense activity. Alternatively, some systems record "events" when a certain threshold of activity is exceeded (examples: another millimeter of precipitation has fallen, another kilometer of wind has moved past, the temperature has changed by a degree, a gust higher than 9.9 m/s has been measured). When this occurs, measurements from all sensors are reported. These measurements are known as "breakpoint" data. In relatively unchanging

69

conditions (long calm periods or rainless weeks, for example), event recorders should send a signal that they are still "alive and well." If systematic recorders are programmed to note and periodically report the highest, lowest, and mean value within each time interval, the likelihood is reduced that interesting behavior will be glossed over or lost. With the capacity of modern data loggers, it is recommended to record and report extremes within the basic time increment (e.g., hourly or 10 minutes). This approach also assists quality-control procedures.

There is usually a trade-off between data volume and time increment, and most automated systems now are set to record approximately hourly. A number of field stations maintained by WRCC are programmed to record in 5- or 10-minute increments, which readily serve to construct an hourly value. However, this approach produces 6–12 times as much data as hourly data. These systems typically do not record details of events at sub-interval time scales, but they easily can record peak values, or counts of threshold exceedance, within the time intervals.

Thus, for each time interval at an automated station, we recommend that several kinds of information—mean or sum, extreme maximum and minimum, and sometimes standard deviation—be recorded. These measurements are useful for quality control and other purposes. Modern data loggers and office computers have quite high capacity. Diagnostic information indicating the state of solar chargers or battery voltages and their extremes is of great value. This topic will be discussed in greater detail in a succeeding section.

Automation also has made possible adaptive or intelligent monitoring techniques where systems vary the recording rate based on detection of the behavior of interest by the software. Sub-interval behavior of interest can be masked on occasion (e.g., a 5-minute extreme downpour with high-erosive capability hidden by an innocuous hourly total). Most users prefer measurements that are systematic in time because they are much easier to summarize and manipulate.

For breakpoint data produced by event reporters, there also is a need to send periodically a signal that the station is still functioning, even though there is nothing more to report. "No report" does not necessarily mean "no data," and it is important to distinguish between the actual observation that was recorded and the content of that observation (e.g., an observation of "0.00" is not the same as "no observation").

E.1.6 Mixed Time Scales

There are times when we may wish to combine information from radically different scales. For example, over the past 100 years we may want to know how the frequency of 5-minute precipitation peaks has varied or how the frequency of peak 1-second wind gusts have varied. We may also want to know over this time if nearby vegetation gradually has grown up to increasingly block the wind or to slowly improve precipitation catch. Answers to these questions require knowledge over a wide range of time scales.

E.1.7 Elements

For manual measurements, the typical elements recorded included temperature extremes, precipitation, and snowfall/snow depth. Automated measurements typically include temperature,

70

precipitation, humidity, wind speed and direction, and solar radiation. An exception to this exists in very windy locations where precipitation is difficult to measure accurately. Automated measurements of snow are improving, but manual measurements are still preferable, as long as shielding is present. Automated measurement of frozen precipitation presents numerous challenges that have not been resolved fully, and the best gauges are quite expensive ($3–8K). Soil temperatures also are included sometimes. Soil moisture is extremely useful, but measurements are not made at many sites. In addition, care must be taken in the installation and maintenance of instruments used in measuring soil moisture. Soil properties vary tremendously in short distances as well, and it is often very difficult ("impossible") to accurately document these variations (without digging up all the soil!). In cooler climates, ultrasonic sensors that detect snow depth are becoming commonplace.

E.1.8 Wind Standards

Wind varies the most in the shortest distance, since it always decreases to zero near the ground and increases rapidly (approximately logarithmically) with height near the ground. Changes in anemometer height obviously will affect distribution of wind speed as will changes in vegetation, obstructions such as buildings, etc. A site that has a 3-m (10-ft) mast clearly will be less windy than a site that has a 6-m (20-ft) or 10-m (33-ft) mast. Historically, many U.S. airports (FAA and NWS) and most current RAWS sites have used a standard 6-m (20-ft) mast for wind measurements. Some NPS RAWS sites utilize shorter masts. Over the last decade, as Automated Surface Observing Systems (ASOSs, mostly NWS) and Automated Weather Observing Systems (AWOSs, mostly FAA) have been deployed at most airports, wind masts have been raised to 8 or 10 m (26 or 33 ft), depending on airplane clearance. The World Meteorological Organization recommends 10 m as the height for wind measurements (WMO 1983; 2005), and more groups are migrating slowly to this standard. The American Association of State Climatologists (AASC 1985) have recommended that wind be measured at 3 m, a standard geared more for agricultural applications than for general purpose uses where higher levels usually are preferred. Different anemometers have different starting thresholds; therefore, areas that frequently experience very light winds may not produce wind measurements thus affecting long-term mean estimates of wind speed. For both sustained winds (averages over a short interval of 2–60 minutes) and especially for gusts, the duration of the sampling interval makes considerable difference. For the same wind history, 1–second gusts are higher than gusts averaging 3 seconds, which in turn are greater than 5-second averages, so that the same sequence would be described with different numbers (all three systems and more are in use). Changes in the averaging procedure, or in height or exposure, can lead to "false" or "fake" climate change with no change in actual climate. Changes in any of these should be noted in the metadata.

E.1.9 Wind Nomenclature

Wind is a vector quantity having a direction and a speed. Directions can be two- or three-dimensional; they will be three-dimensional if the vertical component is important. In all common uses, winds always are denoted by the direction they blow *from* (north wind or southerly breeze). This convention exists because wind often brings weather, and thus our attention is focused upstream. However, this approach contrasts with the way ocean currents are viewed. Ocean currents usually are denoted by the direction they are moving *towards* (eastward current moves from west to east). In specialized applications (such as in atmospheric modeling), wind velocity vectors point in the direction that the wind is blowing. Thus, a southwesterly wind (from the southwest) has both northward and eastward (to the north and to the east) components. Except near mountains, wind cannot blow up or down near the ground, so the vertical component of wind often is approximated as zero, and the horizontal component is emphasized.

E.1.10 Frozen Precipitation

Frozen precipitation is more difficult to measure than liquid precipitation, especially with automated techniques. Goodison et al. (1998), Sevruk and Harmon (1984), Yang et al. (1998, 2001) provide many of the reasons to explain this. The importance of frozen precipitation varies greatly from one setting to another. This subject was discussed in greater detail in a related inventory and monitoring report for the Alaska park units (Redmond et al. 2005).

In climates that receive frozen precipitation, a decision must be made whether or not to try to record such events accurately. This usually means that the precipitation must be turned into liquid either by falling into an antifreeze fluid solution that is then weighed or by heating the precipitation enough to melt and fall through a measuring mechanism such as a nearly-balanced tipping bucket. Accurate measurements from the first approach require expensive gauges; tipping buckets can achieve this resolution readily but are more apt to lose some or all precipitation. Improvements have been made to the heating mechanism on the NWS tipping-bucket gauge used for the ASOS to correct its numerous deficiencies making it less problematic; however, this gauge is not inexpensive. A heat supply needed to melt frozen precipitation usually requires more energy than renewable energy (solar panels or wind recharging) can provide thus AC power is needed. The availability of AC power is severely limited in many cold or remote U. S. settings. Furthermore, periods of frozen precipitation or rime often provide less-than-optimal recharging conditions with heavy clouds, short days, low-solar-elevation angles and more horizon blocking, and cold temperatures causing additional drain on the battery.

E.1.11 Save or Lose

A second consideration with precipitation is determining if the measurement should be saved (as in weighing systems) or lost (as in tipping-bucket systems). With tipping buckets, after the water has passed through the tipping mechanism, it usually just drops to the ground. Thus, there is no checksum to ensure that the sum of all the tips adds up to what has been saved in a reservoir at some location. By contrast, the weighing gauges continually accumulate until the reservoir is emptied, the reported value is the total reservoir content (for example, the height of the liquid column in a tube), and the incremental precipitation is the difference in depth between two known times. These weighing gauges do not always have the same fine resolution. Some gauges only record to the nearest centimeter, which is usually acceptable for hydrology but not necessarily for other needs. (For reference, a millimeter of precipitation can get a person in street clothes quite wet.) This is how the NRCS/USDA SNOTEL system works in climates that measure up to 3000 cm of snow in a winter. (See www.wcc.nrcs.usda.gov/publications for publications or www.wcc.nrcs.usda.gov/factpub/aib536.html for a specific description.) No precipitation is lost this way. A thin layer of oil is used to suppress evaporation, and anti-freeze ensures that frozen precipitation melts. When initially recharged, the sum of the oil and starting antifreeze solution is treated as the zero point. The anti-freeze usually is not sufficiently environmentally friendly to discharge to the ground and thus must be hauled into the area and then back out. Other weighing gauges are capable of measuring to the 0.25-mm (0.01-in.) resolution but do not have as much capacity and must be emptied more often. Day/night and storm-related thermal expansion and contraction and sometimes wind shaking can cause fluid pressure from accumulated totals to go up and down in SNOTEL gauges by small increments (commonly 0.3-3 cm, or 0.01–0.10 ft) leading to "negative precipitation" followed by similarly non-real light precipitation when, in fact, no change took place in the amount of accumulated precipitation.

E.1.12 Time

Time should always be in local standard time (LST), and daylight savings time (DST) should never be used under any circumstances with automated equipment and timers. Using DST leads to one duplicate hour, one missing hour, and a season of displaced values, as well as needless confusion and a data-management nightmare. Absolute time, such as Greenwich Mean Time (GMT) or Coordinated Universal Time (UTC), also can be used because these formats are unambiguously translatable. Since measurements only provide information about what already *has* occurred or *is* occurring and not what *will* occur, they should always be assigned to the *ending time* of the associated interval with hour 24 marking the end of the last hour of the day. In this system, midnight always represents the end of the day, not the start. To demonstrate the importance of this differentiation, we have encountered situations where police officers seeking corroborating weather data could not recall whether the time on their crime report from a year ago was the starting midnight or the ending midnight! Station positions should be known to within a few meters, easily accomplished with GPS, so that time zones and solar angles can be determined accurately.

E.1.13 Automated versus Manual

Most of this report has addressed automated measurements. Historically, most measurements are manual and typically collected once a day. In many cases, manual measurements continue because of habit, usefulness, and desire for continuity over time. Manual measurements are extremely useful and when possible should be encouraged. However, automated measurements are becoming more common. For either, it is important to record time in a logically consistent manner.

It should not be automatically assumed that newer data and measurements are "better" than older data or that manual data are "worse" than automated data. Older or simpler manual measurements are often of very high quality even if they sometimes are not in the most convenient digital format.

There is widespread desire to use automated systems to reduce human involvement. This is admirable and understandable, but every automated weather/climate station or network requires significant human attention and maintenance. A telling example concerns the Oklahoma Mesonet (see Brock et al. 1995, and bibliography at www.mesonet.ou.edu), a network of about 115 high–quality, automated meteorological stations spread over Oklahoma, where about 80 percent of the annual ($2–3M) budget is nonetheless allocated to humans with only about 20 percent allocated to equipment.

E.1.14 Manual Conventions

Manual measurements typically are made once a day. Elements usually consist of maximum and minimum temperature, temperature at observation time, precipitation, snowfall, snow depth, and sometimes evaporation, wind, or other information. Since it is not actually known when extremes occurred, the only logical approach, and the nationwide convention, is to ascribe the entire measurement to the time-interval date and to enter it on the form in that way. For morning observers (for example, 8 am to 8 am), this means that the maximum temperature written for today often is from yesterday afternoon and sometimes the minimum temperature for the 24-hr period actually occurred yesterday morning. However, this is understood and expected. It is often a surprise to observers to see how many maximum temperatures do not occur in the afternoon and how many minimum temperatures do not occur in the predawn hours. This is especially true in environments that are colder, higher, northerly, cloudy, mountainous, or coastal. As long as this convention is strictly followed every day, it has been shown that truly excellent climate records can result (Redmond 1992). Manual observers should reset equipment only one time per day at the official observing time. Making more than one measurement a day is discouraged strongly; this practice results in a hybrid record that is too difficult to interpret. The only exception is for total daily snowfall. New snowfall can be measured up to four times per day with no observations closer than six hours. It is well known that more frequent measurement of snow increases the annual total because compaction is a continuous process.

Two main purposes for climate observations are to establish the long-term averages for given locations and to track variations in climate. Broadly speaking, these purposes address topics of absolute and relative climate behavior. Once absolute behavior has been "established" (a task that is never finished because long-term averages continue to vary in time)—temporal variability quickly becomes the item of most interest.

E.2 Representativeness

Having discussed important factors to consider when new sites are installed, we now turn our attention to site "representativeness." In popular usage, we often encounter the notion that a site is "representative" of another site if it receives the same annual precipitation or records the same annual temperature or if some other element-specific, long-term average has a similar value. This notion of representativeness has a certain limited validity, but there are other aspects of this idea that need to be considered.

A climate monitoring site also can be said to be representative if climate records from that site show sufficiently strong temporal correlations with a large number of locations over a sufficiently large area. If station A receives 20 cm a year and station B receives 200 cm a year, these climates obviously receive quite differing amounts of precipitation. However, if their monthly, seasonal, or annual correlations are high (for example, 0.80 or higher for a particular time scale), one site can be used as a surrogate for estimating values at the other if measurements for a particular month, season, or year are missing. That is, a wet or dry month at one station is also a wet or dry month (relative to its own mean) at the comparison station. Note that high correlations on one time scale do not imply automatically that high correlations will occur on other time scales.

Likewise, two stations having similar mean climates (for example, similar annual precipitation) might not co-vary in close synchrony (for example, coastal versus interior). This may be considered a matter of climate "affiliation" for a particular location.

Thus, the representativeness of a site can refer either to the basic climatic averages for a given duration (or time window within the annual cycle) or to the extent that the site co-varies in time with respect to all surrounding locations. One site can be representative of another in the first sense but not the second, or vice versa, or neither, or both—all combinations are possible.

If two sites are perfectly correlated then, in a sense, they are "redundant." However, redundancy has value because all sites will experience missing data especially with automated equipment in rugged environments and harsh climates where outages and other problems nearly can be guaranteed. In many cases, those outages are caused by the weather, particularly by unusual weather and the very conditions we most wish to know about. Methods for filling in those values will require proxy information from this or other nearby networks. Thus, redundancy is a virtue rather than a vice.

In general, the cooperative stations managed by the NWS have produced much longer records than automated stations like RAWS or SNOTEL stations. The RAWS stations often have problems with precipitation, especially in winter, or with missing data, so that low correlations may be data problems rather than climatic dissimilarity. The RAWS records also are relatively short, so correlations should be interpreted with care. In performing and interpreting such analyses, however, we must remember that there are physical climate reasons and observational reasons why stations within a short distance (even a few tens or hundreds of meters) may not correlate well.

E.2.1 Temporal Behavior

It is possible that high correlations will occur between station pairs during certain portions of the year (i.e., January) but low correlations may occur during other portions of the year (e.g., September or October). The relative contributions of these seasons to the annual total (for precipitation) or average (for temperature) and the correlations for each month are both factors in the correlation of an aggregated time window of longer duration that encompasses those seasons (e.g., one of the year definitions such as calendar year or water year). A complete and careful evaluation ideally would include such a correlation analysis but requires more resources and data. Note that it also is possible and frequently is observed that temperatures are highly correlated while precipitation is not or vice versa, and these relations can change according to the time of year. If two stations are well correlated for all climate elements for all portions of the year, then they can be considered redundant.

With scarce resources, the initial strategy should be to try to identify locations that do not correlate particularly well, so that each new site measures something new that cannot be guessed easily from the behavior of surrounding sites. (An important caveat here is that lack of such correlation could be a result of physical climate behavior and not a result of faults with the actual measuring process; i.e., by unrepresentative or simply poor-quality data. Unfortunately, we seldom have perfect climate data.) As additional sites are added, we usually wish for some combination of unique and redundant sites to meet what amounts to essentially orthogonal constraints: new information and more reliably-furnished information.

A common consideration is whether to observe on a ridge or in a valley, given the resources to place a single station within a particular area of a few square kilometers. Ridge and valley stations will correlate very well for temperatures when lapse conditions prevail, particularly summer daytime temperatures. In summer at night or winter at daylight, the picture will be more mixed and correlations will be lower. In winter at night when inversions are common and even the rule, correlations may be zero or even negative and perhaps even more divergent as the two sites are on opposite sides of the inversion. If we had the luxury of locating stations everywhere, we would find that ridge tops generally correlate very well with other ridge tops and similarly valleys with other valleys, but ridge tops correlate well with valleys only under certain circumstances. Beyond this, valleys and ridges having similar orientations usually will correlate better with each other than those with perpendicular orientations, depending on their orientation with respect to large-scale wind flow and solar angles.

Unfortunately, we do not have stations everywhere, so we are forced to use the few comparisons that we have and include a large dose of intelligent reasoning, using what we have observed elsewhere. In performing and interpreting such analyses, we must remember that there are physical climatic reasons and observational reasons why stations within a short distance (even a few tens or hundreds of meters) may not correlate well.

Examples of correlation analyses include those for the Channel Islands and for southwest Alaska, which can be found in Redmond and McCurdy (2005) and Redmond et al. (2005). These examples illustrate what can be learned from correlation analyses. Spatial correlations generally vary by time of year. Thus, results should be displayed in the form of annual correlation cycles—for monthly mean temperature and monthly total precipitation and perhaps other climate elements like wind or humidity—between station pairs selected for climatic setting and data availability and quality.

In general, the COOP stations managed by the NWS have produced much longer records than have automated stations like RAWS or SNOTEL stations. The RAWS stations also often have problems with precipitation, especially in winter or with missing data, so that low correlations may be data problems rather than climate dissimilarity. The RAWS records are much shorter, so correlations should be interpreted with care, but these stations are more likely to be in places of interest for remote or under-sampled regions.

E.2.2 Spatial Behavior

76

A number of techniques exist to interpolate from isolated point values to a spatial domain. For example, a common technique is simple inverse distance weighting. Critical to the success of the simplest of such techniques is that some other property of the spatial domain, one that is influential for the mapped element, does not vary significantly. Topography greatly influences precipitation, temperature, wind, humidity, and most other meteorological elements. Thus, this criterion clearly is not met in any region having extreme topographic diversity. In such circumstances, simple Cartesian distance may have little to do with how rapidly correlation deteriorates from one site to the next, and in fact, the correlations can decrease readily from a mountain to a valley and then increase again on the next mountain. Such structure in the fields of spatial correlation is not seen in the relatively (statistically) well-behaved flat areas like those in the eastern United States.

To account for dominating effects such as topography and inland–coastal differences that exist in certain regions, some kind of additional knowledge must be brought to bear to produce meaningful, physically plausible, and observationally based interpolations. Historically, this has proven to be an extremely difficult problem, especially to perform objective and repeatable analyses. An analysis performed for southwest Alaska (Redmond et al. 2005) concluded that the PRISM (Parameter Regression on Independent Slopes Model) maps (Daly et al. 1994, 2002; Gibson et al., 2002; Doggett et al., 2004) were probably the best available. An analysis by Simpson et al. (2005) further discussed many issues in the mapping of Alaska's climate and resulted in the same conclusion about PRISM.

E.2.3 Climate-Change Detection

Although general purpose climate stations should be situated to address all aspects of climate variability, it is desirable that they also be in locations that are more sensitive to climate change from natural or anthropogenic influences should it begin to occur. The question here is how well we know such sensitivities. The polar regions and especially the North Pole are generally regarded as being more sensitive to changes in radiative forcing of climate because of positive feedbacks. The climate-change issue is quite complex because it encompasses more than just greenhouse gasses.

Sites that are in locations or climates particularly vulnerable to climate change should be favored. How this vulnerability is determined is a considerably challenging research issue. Candidate locations or situations are those that lie on the border between two major biomes or just inside the edge of one or the other. In these cases, a slight movement of the boundary in anticipated direction (toward "warmer," for example) would be much easier to detect as the boundary moves past the site and a different set of biota begin to be established. Such a vegetative or ecologic response would be more visible and would take less time to establish as a real change than would a smaller change in the center of the distribution range of a marker or key species.

E.2.4 Element-Specific Differences

The various climate elements (temperature, precipitation, cloudiness, snowfall, humidity, wind speed and direction, solar radiation) do not vary through time in the same sequence or manner nor should they necessarily be expected to vary in this manner. The spatial patterns of variability should not be expected to be the same for all elements. These patterns also should not be expected to be similar for all months or seasons. The suitability of individual sites for measurement also varies from one element to another. A site that has a favorable exposure for temperature or wind may not have a favorable exposure for precipitation or snowfall. A site that experiences proper air movement may be situated in a topographic channel, such as a river valley or a pass, which restricts the range of wind directions and affects the distribution of speed-direction categories.

E.2.5 Logistics and Practical Factors

Even with the most advanced scientific rationale, sites in some remote or climatically challenging settings may not be suitable because of the difficulty in servicing and maintaining equipment. Contributing to these challenges are scheduling difficulties, animal behavior, snow burial, icing, snow behavior, access and logistical problems, and the weather itself. Remote and elevated sites usually require far more attention and expense than a rain-dominated, easily accessible valley location.

For climate purposes, station exposure and the local environment should be maintained in their original state (vegetation especially), so that changes seen are the result of regional climate variations and not of trees growing up, bushes crowding a site, surface albedo changing, fire clearing, etc. Repeat photography has shown many examples of slow environmental change in the vicinity of a station in rather short time frames (5–20 years), and this technique should be employed routinely and frequently at all locations. In the end, logistics, maintenance, and other practical factors almost always determine the success of weather- and climate-monitoring activities.

E.2.6 Personnel Factors

Many past experiences (almost exclusively negative) strongly support the necessity to place primary responsibility for station deployment and maintenance in the hands of seasoned, highly qualified, trained, and meticulously careful personnel, the more experienced the better. Over time, even in "benign" climates but especially where harsher conditions prevail, every conceivable problem will occur and both the usual and unusual should be anticipated: weather, animals, plants, salt, sensor and communication failure, windblown debris, corrosion, power failures, vibrations, avalanches, snow loading and creep, corruption of the data logger program, etc. An ability to anticipate and forestall such problems, a knack for innovation and improvisation, knowledge of electronics, practical and organizational skills, and presence of mind to bring the various small but vital parts, spares, tools, and diagnostic troubleshooting equipment are highly valued qualities. Especially when logistics are so expensive, a premium should be placed on using experienced personnel, since the slightest and seemingly most minor mistake can render a station useless or, even worse, uncertain. Exclusive reliance on individuals without this background can be costly and almost always will result eventually in unnecessary loss of data. Skilled labor and an apprenticeship system to develop new skilled labor will greatly reduce (but not eliminate) the types of problems that can occur in operating a climate network.

E.3 Site Selection

In addition to considerations identified previously in this appendix, various factors need to be considered in selecting sites for new or augmented instrumentation.

E.3.1 Equipment and Exposure Factors

E.3.1.1 Measurement Suite: All sites should measure temperature, humidity, wind, solar radiation, and snow depth. Precipitation measurements are more difficult but probably should be attempted with the understanding that winter measurements may be of limited or no value unless an all-weather gauge has been installed. Even if an all-weather gauge has been installed, it is desirable to have a second gauge present that operates on a different principle–for example, a fluid-based system like those used in the SNOTEL stations in tandem with a higher–resolution, tipping bucket gauge for summertime. Without heating, a tipping bucket gauge usually is of use only when temperatures are above freezing and when temperatures have not been below freezing for some time, so that accumulated ice and snow is not melting and being recorded as present precipitation. Gauge undercatch is a significant issue in snowy climates, so shielding should be considered for all gauges designed to work over the winter months. It is very important to note the presence or absence of shielding, the type of shielding, and the dates of installation or removal of the shielding.

E.3.1.2 Overall Exposure: The ideal, general all-purpose site has gentle slopes, is open to the sun and the wind, has a natural vegetative cover, avoids strong local (less than 200 m) influences, and represents a reasonable compromise among all climate elements. The best temperature sites are not the best precipitation sites, and the same is true for other elements. Steep topography in the immediate vicinity should be avoided unless settings where precipitation is affected by steep topography are being deliberately sought or a mountaintop or ridgeline is the desired location. The potential for disturbance should be considered: fire and flood risk, earth movement, wind-borne debris, volcanic deposits or lahars, vandalism, animal tampering, and general human encroachment are all factors.

E.3.1.3 Elevation: Mountain climates do not vary in time in exactly the same manner as adjoining valley climates. This concept is emphasized when temperature inversions are present to a greater degree and during precipitation when winds rise up the slopes at the same angle. There is considerable concern that mountain climates will be (or already are) changing and perhaps changing differently than lowland climates, which has direct and indirect consequences for plant and animal life in the more extreme zones. Elevations of special significance are those that are near the mean rain/snow line for winter, near the tree line, and near the mean annual freezing level (all of these may not be quite the same). Because the lapse rates in wet climates often are nearly moist-adiabatic during the main precipitation seasons, measurements at one elevation may be extrapolated to nearby elevations. In drier climates and in the winter, temperature and to a lesser extent wind will show various elevation profiles.

E.3.1.4 Transects: The concept of observing transects that span climatic gradients is sound. This is not always straightforward in topographically uneven terrain, but these transects could still be arranged by setting up station(s) along the coast; in or near passes atop the main coastal interior drainage divide; and inland at one, two, or three distances into the interior lowlands. Transects need not—and by dint of topographic constraints probably cannot—be straight lines, but the closer that a line can be approximated the better. The main point is to systematically sample the key points of a behavioral transition without deviating too radically from linearity.

E.3.1.5 Other Topographic Considerations: There are various considerations with respect to local topography. Local topography can influence wind (channeling, upslope/downslope, etc.), precipitation (orographic enhancement, downslope evaporation, catch efficiency, etc.), and temperature (frost pockets, hilltops, aspect, mixing or decoupling from the overlying atmosphere, bowls, radiative effects, etc.), to different degrees at differing scales. In general, for measurements to be areally representative, it is better to avoid these local effects to the extent that they can be identified before station deployment (once deployed, it is desirable not to move a station). The primary purpose of a climate-monitoring network should be to serve as an infrastructure in the form of a set of benchmark stations for comparing other stations. Sometimes, however, it is exactly these local phenomena that we want to capture. Living organisms, especially plants, are affected by their immediate environment, whether it is representative of a larger setting or not. Specific measurements of limited scope and duration made for these purposes then can be tied to the main benchmarks. This experience is useful also in determining the complexity needed in the benchmark monitoring process in order to capture particular phenomena at particular space and time scales.

Sites that drain (cold air) well generally are better than sites that allow cold air to pool. Slightly sloped areas (1 degree is fine) or small benches from tens to hundreds of meters above streams are often favorable locations. Furthermore, these sites often tend to be out of the path of hazards (like floods) and to have rocky outcroppings where controlling vegetation will not be a major concern. Benches or wide spots on the rise between two forks of a river system are often the only flat areas and sometimes jut out to give greater exposure to winds from more directions.

E.3.1.6 Prior History: The starting point in designing a program is to determine what kinds of observations have been collected over time, by whom, in what manner, and if these observation are continuing to the present time. It also may be of value to "re-occupy" the former site of a station that is now inactive to provide some measure of continuity or a reference point from the past. This can be of value even if continuous observations were not made during the entire intervening period.

E.3.2 Element-Specific Factors

E.3.2.1 Temperature: An open exposure with uninhibited air movement is the preferred setting. The most common measurement is made at approximately eye level, 1.5–2.0 m. In snowy locations sensors should be at least one meter higher than the deepest snowpack expected in the next 50 years or perhaps 2–3 times the depth of the average maximum annual depth. Sensors should be shielded above and below from solar radiation (bouncing off snow), from sunrise/sunset horizontal input, and from vertical rock faces. Sensors should be clamped tightly, so that they do not swivel away from level stacks of radiation plates. Nearby vegetation should be kept away from the sensors (several meters). Growing vegetation should be cut to original conditions. Small hollows and swales can cool tremendously at night, and it is best avoid these areas. Side slopes of perhaps a degree or two of angle facilitate air movement and drainage and, in effect, sample a large area during nighttime hours. The very bottom of a valley should be avoided. Temperature can change substantially from moves of only a few meters. Situations have been observed where flat and seemingly uniform conditions (like airport runways) appear to demonstrate different climate behaviors over short distances of a few tens or hundreds of meters (differences of 5–10°C). When snow is on the ground, these microclimatic differences can be stronger, and differences of 2–5°C can occur in the short distance between the thermometer and the snow surface on calm evenings.

E.3.2.2 Precipitation (liquid): Calm locations with vegetative or artificial shielding are preferred. Wind will adversely impact readings; therefore, the less the better. Wind effects on precipitation are far less for rain than for snow. Devices that "save" precipitation present advantages, but most gauges are built to dump precipitation as it falls or to empty periodically. Automated gauges give both the amount and the timing. Simple backups that record only the total precipitation since the last visit have a certain advantage (for example, storage gauges or lengths of PVC pipe perhaps with bladders on the bottom). The following question should be asked: Does the total precipitation from an automated gauge add up to the measured total in a simple bucket (evaporation is prevented with an appropriate substance such as mineral oil)? Drip from overhanging foliage and trees can augment precipitation totals.

E.3.2.3 Precipitation (frozen): Calm locations or shielding are a must. Undercatch for rain is only about 5 percent, but with winds of only 2–4 m/s, gauges may catch only 30–70 percent of the actual snow falling depending on density of the flakes. To catch 100 percent of the snow, the standard configuration for shielding is employed by the CRN (Climate Reference Network): the DFIR (Double-Fence Intercomparison Reference) shield with 2.4-m (8-ft.) vertical, wooden slatted fences in two concentric octagons with diameters of 8 m and 4 m (26 ft and 13 ft, respectively) and an inner Alter shield (flapping vanes). Numerous tests have shown this is the only way to achieve complete catch of snowfall (e.g., Yang et al. 1998, 2001). The DFIR shield is large and bulky; it is recommended that all precipitation gauges have at least Alter shields on them.

Near the coast, much snow is heavy and falls more vertically. In colder locations or storms, light flakes frequently will fly in and then out of the gauge. Clearings in forests are usually excellent sites. Snow blowing from trees that are too close can augment actual precipitation totals. Artificial shielding (vanes, etc.) placed around gauges in snowy locales always should be used if accurate totals are desired. Moving parts tend to freeze up. Capping of gauges during heavy snowfall events is a common occurrence. When the cap becomes pointed, snow falls off to the ground and is not recorded. Caps and plugs often will not fall into the tube until hours, days, or even weeks have passed, typically during an extended period of freezing temperature or above or when sunlight finally occurs. Liquid-based measurements (e.g., SNOTEL "rocket" gauges) do not have the resolution (usually 0.3 cm [0.1 in.] rather than 0.03 cm [0.01 in.]) that tipping bucket and other gauges have but are known to be reasonably accurate in very snowy climates. Light snowfall events might not be recorded until enough of them add up to the next reporting increment. More expensive gauges like Geonors can be considered and could do quite well in snowy settings; however, they need to be emptied every 40 cm (15 in.) or so (capacity of 51 cm [20 in.]) until the new 91-cm (36-in.) capacity gauge is offered for sale. Recently, the NWS has been trying out the new (and very expensive) Ott all-weather gauge. Riming can be an issue in windy foggy environments below freezing. Rime, dew, and other forms of atmospheric condensation are not real precipitation, since they are caused by the gauge.

E.3.2.4 Snow Depth: Windswept areas tend to be blown clear of snow. Conversely, certain types of vegetation can act as a snow fence and cause artificial drifts. However, some amount of vegetation in the vicinity generally can help slow down the wind. The two most common types of snow-depth gauges are the Judd Snow Depth Sensor, produced by Judd Communications, and the snow depth gauge produced by Campbell Scientific, Inc. Opinions vary on which one is better. These gauges use ultrasound and look downward in a cone about 22 degrees in diameter. The ground should be relatively clear of vegetation and maintained in a manner so that the zero point on the calibration scale does not change.

E.3.2.5 Snow Water Equivalent: This is determined by the weight of snow on fluid-filled pads about the size of a desktop set up sometimes in groups of four or in larger hexagons several meters in diameter. These pads require flat ground some distance from nearby sources of windblown snow and shielding that is "just right": not too close to the shielding to act as a kind of snow fence and not too far from the shielding so that blowing and drifting become a factor. Generally, these pads require fluids that possess antifreeze-like properties, as well as handling and replacement protocols.

E.3.2.6 Wind: Open exposures are needed for wind measurements. Small prominences or benches without blockage from certain sectors are preferred. A typical rule for trees is to site stations back 10 tree-heights from all tree obstructions. Sites in long, narrow valleys can obviously only exhibit two main wind directions. Gently rounded eminences are more favored. Any kind of topographic steering should be avoided to the extent possible. Avoiding major mountain chains or single isolated mountains or ridges is usually a favorable approach, if there is a choice. Sustained wind speed and the highest gusts (1-second) should be recorded. Averaging methodologies for both sustained winds and gusts can affect climate trends and should be recorded as metadata with all changes noted. Vegetation growth affects the vertical wind profile, and growth over a few years can lead to changes in mean wind speed even if the "real" wind does not change, so vegetation near the site (perhaps out to 50 m) should be maintained in a quasi-permanent status (same height and spatial distribution). Wind devices can rime up and freeze or spin out of balance. In severely rimed or windy climates, rugged anemometers, such as those made by Taylor, are worth considering. These anemometers are expensive but durable and can withstand substantial abuse. In exposed locations, personnel should plan for winds to be at least 50 m/s and be able to measure these wind speeds. At a minimum, anemometers should be rated to 75 m/s.

E.3.2.7 Humidity: Humidity is a relatively straightforward climate element. Close proximity to lakes or other water features can affect readings. Humidity readings typically are less accurate near 100 percent and at low humidities in cold weather.

E.3.2.8 Solar Radiation: A site with an unobstructed horizon obviously is the most desirable. This generally implies a flat plateau or summit. However, in most locations trees or mountains will obstruct the sun for part of the day.

E.3.2.9 Soil Temperature: It is desirable to measure soil temperature at locations where soil is present. If soil temperature is recorded at only a single depth, the most preferred depth is 10 cm. Other common depths include 25 cm, 50 cm, 2 cm, and 100 cm. Biological activity in the soil will be proportional to temperature with important threshold effects occurring near freezing.

E.3.2.10 Soil Moisture: Soil-moisture gauges are somewhat temperamental and require care to install. The soil should be characterized by a soil expert during installation of the gauge. The readings may require a certain level of experience to interpret correctly. If accurate, readings of soil moisture are especially useful.

E.3.2.11 Distributed Observations: It can be seen readily that compromises must be struck among the considerations described in the preceding paragraphs because some are mutually exclusive.

How large can a "site" be? Generally, the equipment footprint should be kept as small as practical with all components placed next to each other (within less than 10–20 m or so). Readings from one instrument frequently are used to aid in interpreting readings from the remaining instruments.

What is a tolerable degree of separation? Some consideration may be given to locating a precipitation gauge or snow pillow among protective vegetation, while the associated temperature, wind, and humidity readings would be collected more effectively in an open and exposed location within 20–50 m. Ideally, it is advantageous to know the wind measurement precisely at the precipitation gauge, but a compromise involving a short split, and in effect a "distributed observation," could be considered. There are no definitive rules governing this decision, but it is suggested that the site footprint be kept within approximately 50 m. There also are constraints imposed by engineering and electrical factors that affect cable lengths, signal strength, and line noise; therefore, the shorter the cable the better. Practical issues include the need to trench a channel to outlying instruments or to allow lines to lie atop the ground and associated problems with animals, humans, weathering, etc. Separating a precipitation gauge up to 100 m or so from an instrument mast may be an acceptable compromise if other factors are not limiting.

E.3.2.12 Instrument Replacement Schedules: Instruments slowly degrade, and a plan for replacing them with new, refurbished, or recalibrated instruments should be in place. After approximately five years, a systematic change-out procedure should result in replacing most sensors in a network. Certain parts, such as solar radiation sensors, are candidates for annual calibration or change-out. Anemometers tend to degrade as bearings erode or electrical contacts become uneven. Noisy bearings are an indication, and a stethoscope might aid in hearing such noises. Increased internal friction affects the threshold starting speed; once spinning, they tend to function properly. Increases in starting threshold speeds can lead to more zero-wind measurements and thus reduce the reported mean wind speed with no real change in wind properties. A field calibration kit should be developed and taken on all site visits, routine or otherwise. Rain gauges can be tested with drip testers during field visits. Protective conduit and tight water seals can prevent abrasion and moisture problems with the equipment, although seals can keep moisture in as well as out. Bulletproof casings sometimes are employed in remote settings. A supply of spare parts, at least one of each and more for less-expensive or more-delicate sensors, should be maintained to allow replacement of worn or nonfunctional instruments during field visits. In addition, this approach allows instruments to be calibrated in the relative convenience of the operational home—the larger the network, the greater the need for a parts depot.

E.3.3 Long-Term Comparability and Consistency

E.3.3.1 Consistency: The emphasis here is to hold biases constant. Every site has biases, problems, and idiosyncrasies of one sort or another. The best rule to follow is simply to try to keep biases constant through time. Since the goal is to track climate through time, keeping sensors, methodologies, and exposure constant will ensure that only true climate change is being measured. This means leaving the site in its original state or performing maintenance to keep it that way. Once a site is installed, the goal should be to never move the site even by a few meters or to allow significant changes to occur within 100 m for the next several decades.

Sites in or near rock outcroppings likely will experience less vegetative disturbance or growth through the years and will not usually retain moisture, a factor that could speed corrosion. Sites that will remain locally similar for some time are usually preferable. However, in some cases the intent of a station might be to record the local climate effects of changes within a small-scale system (for example, glacier, recently burned area, or scene of some other disturbance) that is subject to a regional climate influence. In this example, the local changes might be much larger than the regional changes.

E.3.3.2 Metadata: Since the climate of every site is affected by features in the immediate vicinity, it is vital to record this information over time and to update the record repeatedly at each service visit. Distances, angles, heights of vegetation, fine-scale topography, condition of instruments, shielding discoloration, and other factors from within a meter to several kilometers should be noted. Systematic photography should be undertaken and updated at least once every one–two years.

Photographic documentation should be taken at each site in a standard manner and repeated every two–three years. Guidelines for methodology were developed by Redmond (2004) as a result of experience with the NOAA CRN and can be found on the WRCC NPS Web pages at www.wrcc.dri.edu/nps and at ftp.wrcc.dri.edu/nps/photodocumentation.pdf.

The main purpose for climate stations is to *track climatic conditions through time*. Anything that affects the interpretation of records through time must to be noted and recorded for posterity. The important factors should be clear to a person who has never visited the site, no matter how long ago the site was installed.

In regions with significant, climatic transition zones, transects are an efficient way to span several climates and make use of available resources. Discussions on this topic at greater detail can be found in Redmond and Simeral (2004) and in Redmond et al. (2005).

E.4 Literature Cited

American Association of State Climatologists. 1985. Heights and Exposure Standards for Sensors on Automated Weather Stations. The State Climatologist **9**(4).

Brock, F. V., K. C. Crawford, R. L. Elliott, G. W. Cuperus, S. J. Stadler, H. L. Johnson and M. D. Eilts. 1995. The Oklahoma Mesonet: A Technical Overview. Journal of Atmospheric and Oceanic Technology **12**:5-19.

Daly, C., R. P. Neilson, and D. L. Phillips. 1994. A Statistical-Topographic Model for Mapping Climatological Precipitation over Mountainous Terrain. Journal of Applied Meteorology **33**:140-158.

Daly, C., W. P. Gibson, G. H. Taylor, G. L. Johnson, and P. Pasteris. 2002. A knowledge-based approach to the statistical mapping of climate. Climate Research **22**:99-113.

Doggett, M., C. Daly, J. Smith, W. Gibson, G. Taylor, G. Johnson, and P. Pasteris. 2004. High-resolution 1971-2000 mean monthly temperature maps for the western United States. Fourteenth AMS Conf. on Applied Climatology, 84th AMS Annual Meeting. Seattle, WA, American Meteorological Society, Boston, MA, January 2004, Paper 4.3, CD-ROM.

Geiger, R., R. H. Aron, and P. E. Todhunter. 2003. The Climate Near the Ground. 6th edition. Rowman & Littlefield Publishers, Inc., New York.

Gibson, W. P., C. Daly, T. Kittel, D. Nychka, C. Johns, N. Rosenbloom, A. McNab, and G. Taylor. 2002. Development of a 103-year high-resolution climate data set for the conterminous United States. Thirteenth AMS Conf. on Applied Climatology. Portland, OR, American Meteorological Society, Boston, MA, May 2002:181-183.

Goodison, B. E., P. Y. T. Louie, and D. Yang. 1998. WMO Solid Precipitation Measurement Intercomparison Final Report. WMO TD 982, World Meteorological Organization, Geneva, Switzerland.

National Research Council. 1998. Future of the National Weather Service Cooperative Weather Network. National Academies Press, Washington, D.C.

National Research Council. 2001. A Climate Services Vision: First Steps Toward the Future. National Academies Press, Washington, D.C.

Redmond, K. T. 1992. Effects of observation time on interpretation of climatic time series - A need for consistency. Eighth Annual Pacific Climate (PACLIM) Workshop. Pacific Grove, CA, March 1991:141-150.

Redmond, K. T. 2004. Photographic Documentation of Long-Term Climate Stations. Available from ftp://ftp.wrcc.dri.edu/nps/photodocumentation.pdf. (accessed 15 August 2004)

Redmond, K. T. and D. B. Simeral. 2004. Climate Monitoring Comments: Central Alaska Network Inventory and Monitoring Program. Available from ftp://ftp.wrcc.dri.edu/nps/alaska/cakn/npscakncomments040406.pdf (accessed 6 April 2004).

Redmond, K. T., D. B. Simeral, and G. D. McCurdy. 2005. Climate Monitoring for Southwest Alaska National Parks: Network Design and Site Selection. Report 05-01. Western Regional Climate Center, Reno, Nevada.

Redmond, K. T., and G. D. McCurdy. 2005. Channel Islands National Park: Design considerations for Weather and Climate Monitoring. Report 05-02. Western Regional Climate Center, Reno, Nevada.

Sevruk, B., and W. R. Hamon. 1984. International comparison of national precipitation gauges with a reference pit gauge. Instruments and Observing Methods, Report No 17, WMO/TD – 38, World Meteorological Organization, Geneva, Switzerland.

Simpson, J. J., Hufford, G. L., C. Daly, J. S. Berg, and M. D. Fleming. 2005. Comparing maps of mean monthly surface temperature and precipitation for Alaska and adjacent areas of Canada produced by two different methods. Arctic **58**(2):137-161.

Whiteman, C. D. 2000. Mountain Meteorology: Fundamentals and Applications. Oxford University Press, Oxford, UK.

Wilson, E. O. 1998. Consilience: The Unity of Knowledge. Knopf, New York.

World Meteorological Organization. 1983. Guide to Meteorological Instruments and Methods of Observation, No. 8, 5th edition, World Meteorological Organization, Geneva Switzerland.

World Meteorological Organization. 2005. Organization and planning of intercomparisons of rainfall intensity gauges. World Meteorological Organization, Geneva Switzerland.

Yang, D., B. E. Goodison, J. R. Metcalfe, V. S. Golubev, R. Bates, T. Pangburn, and C. Hanson. 1998. Accuracy of NWS 8" Standard Nonrecording Precipitation Gauge: Results and Application of WMO Intercomparison. Journal of Atmospheric and Oceanic Technology **15**(2):54-68.

Yang, D., B. E. Goodison, J. R. Metcalfe, P. Louie, E. Elomaa, C. Hanson, V. Bolubev, T. Gunther, J. Milkovic, and M. Lapin. 2001. Compatibility evaluation of national precipitation gauge measurements. Journal of Geophysical Research **106**(D2):1481-1491.

Appendix F. Descriptions of weather/climate monitoring networks.

F.1 Clean Air Status and Trends Network (CASTNet)

- Purpose of network: provide information for evaluating the effectiveness of national emission-control strategies.
- Primary management agency: EPA.
- Data website: http://epa.gov/castnet/.
- Measured weather/climate elements:
  o Air temperature.
  o Precipitation.
  o Relative humidity.
  o Wind speed.
  o Wind direction.
  o Wind gust.
  o Gust direction.
  o Solar radiation.
  o Soil moisture and temperature.
- Sampling frequency: hourly.
- Reporting frequency: hourly.
- Estimated station cost: $13K.
- Network strengths:
  o High-quality data.
  o Sites are well maintained.
- Network weaknesses:
  o Density of station coverage is low.
  o Shorter periods of record for western United States.

CASTNet primarily is an air-quality-monitoring network managed by the EPA. The elements shown here are intended to support interpretation of measured air-quality parameters such as ozone, nitrates, sulfides, etc., which also are measured at CASTNet sites.

F.2 NOAA Coastal Marine Automated Network (C-MAN)

- Purpose of network: Shore-based measurement of atmospheric elements in a marine environment for maritime uses and for analysis, diagnosis, and forecasting.
- Primary management agency: National Data Buoy Center (NDBC).
- Data website: http://www.ndbc.noaa.gov.
- Measured weather/climate elements:
  o Air temperature.
  o Relative humidity (some sites).
  o Precipitation (some sites).
  o Barometric pressure.
  o Wind direction, speed, gusts.
  o Water temperature (some sites).

- o Water level (some sites).
- o Wave information (some sites).
- o Visibility (some sites).
- Sampling frequency: hourly.
- Reporting frequency: hourly.
- Estimated station cost: unknown.
- Network strengths:
  - o Gives information from unique locations, difficult to find otherwise.
  - o Stations are located at ocean/land transition.
  - o Sites are well maintained.
  - o Standard meteorological measurements with fine time resolution.
  - o High-quality site exposures.
  - o Accessible data.
- Network weaknesses:
  - o Relatively few stations.
  - o Records are no longer than 20 years.

These stations supplanted the old Coast Guard stations at lighthouses, at capes and beaches, on near shore islands, and on offshore platforms. The Coast Guard sites were modernized under LAMPS (Lighthouse Automation and Modernization Program) starting in the early 1980s. There are currently 69 C-MAN sites (2006), with 9 in Alaska, and 8 of those near Cook Inlet and Prince William Sound. WRCC has obtained all historical C-MAN data and provides access to it.

F.3 NWS Cooperative Observer Program (COOP)

- Purpose of network:
  - o Provide observational, meteorological data required to define U.S. climate and help measure long-term climate changes.
  - o Provide observational, meteorological data in near real-time to support forecasting and warning mechanisms and other public service programs of the NWS.
- Primary management agency: NOAA (NWS).
- Data website: data are available from the NCDC (www.ncdc.noaa.gov), RCCs (e.g., WRCC, www.wrcc.dri.edu), and state climate offices.
- Measured weather/climate elements
  - o Maximum, minimum, and observation-time temperature.
  - o Precipitation, snowfall, snow depth.
  - o Pan evaporation (some stations).
- Sampling frequency: daily.
- Reporting frequency: daily or monthly (station-dependent).
- Estimated station cost: $2K with maintenance costs of $500–900/year.
- Network strengths:
  - o Decade–century records at most sites.
  - o Widespread national coverage (thousands of stations).
  - o Excellent data quality when well maintained.
  - o Relatively inexpensive; highly cost effective.
  - o Manual measurements; not automated.
- Network weaknesses:

90

o Uneven exposures; many are not well-maintained.

o Dependence on schedules for volunteer observers.

o Slow entry of data from many stations into national archives.

o Data subject to observational methodology; not always documented.

o Manual measurements; not automated and not hourly.

The COOP network has long served as the main climate observation network in the United States. Readings are usually made by volunteers using equipment supplied, installed, and maintained by the federal government. The observer in effect acts as a host for the data-gathering activities and supplies the labor; this is truly a "cooperative" effort. The SAO sites often are considered to be part of the cooperative network as well if they collect the previously mentioned types of weather/climate observations. Typical observation days are morning to morning, evening to evening, or midnight to midnight. By convention, observations are ascribed to the date the instrument was reset at the end of the observational period. For this reason, midnight observations represent the end of a day. The Historical Climate Network is a subset of the cooperative network but contains longer and more complete records.

F.4 NPS Gaseous Pollutant Monitoring Program (GPMP)

- Purpose of network: measurement of ozone and related meteorological elements.
- Primary management agency: NPS.
- Data website: http://www2.nature.nps.gov/air/monitoring.
- Measured weather/climate elements:
  o Air temperature.
  o Relative humidity
  o Precipitation.
  o Wind speed and direction.
  o Solar radiation.
  o Surface wetness
- Sampling frequency: continuous.
- Reporting frequency: hourly.
- Estimated station cost: unknown.
- Network strengths:
  o Stations are located within NPS park units.
  o Data quality is excellent, with high data standards.
  o Provides unique measurements that are not available elsewhere.
  o Records are up to 2 decades in length.
  o Site maintenance is excellent.
  o Thermometers are aspirated.
- Network weaknesses:
  o Not easy to download the entire data set or to ingest live data.
  o Period of record is short compared to other automated networks. Earliest sites date from 2004.
  o Station spacing and coverage: station installation is episodic, driven by opportunistic situations.

The NPS web site indicates that there are 33 sites with continuous ozone analysis run by NPS, with records from a few to about 16-17 years. Of these stations, 12 are labeled as GPMP sites and the rest are labeled as CASTNet sites. All of these have standard meteorological measurements, including a 10-m mast. Another 9 GPMP sites are located within NPS units but run by cooperating agencies. A number of other sites (1-2 dozen) ran for differing periods in the past, generally less than 5-10 years.

F.5 Regional network. Denali Rock Creek (I&M)

- Purpose of network: provide climate observations for the LTEM program in DENA.
- Primary management agency: NPS.
- Data website: unknown.
- Measured weather/climate elements:
    o Air temperature.
    o Precipitation.
    o Wind speed and direction.
    o Solar radiation.
- Sampling frequency: hourly.
- Reporting frequency: hourly, to an on-site datalogger.
- Estimated station cost: unknown.
- Network strengths:
    o Local observations for DENA.
    o Network is dense and covers a range of elevations in a local area.
    o Fine temporal resolution.
- Network weaknesses:
    o Data are not readily accessible via the Internet.
    o Metadata are not readily accessible.

A small network of five automated stations in Denali was set up in 1994 as part of the LTEM network. These stations are located at different elevations within a single watershed adjacent to park headquarters. The following information was adapted from the NASA Global Change Master Directory:

Sites cover four major vegetation communities and ecotones. A soil inventory and soil characterization sampling were conducted with cooperation from the USDA / NRCS Alaska State Office. Complete soil analyses were performed by NRCS - National Soil Survey Center according to national cooperative soil survey procedures and standards. The soil characterization provides baseline data for soil parameters and also reference points for future changes in these parameters. Soil elements monitored include: soil temperature (2.5, 5, 10, 20, 50 cm, and 100 cm for deep soils), soil redox potential, soil water table, and soil matrix water potential (daily at 5, 10, 20, 50, 75 cm with synthetic moisture blocks). Other elements include hourly air temperature, relative humidity, wind, and solar radiation. Reduction-oxidation potential (redox) potential measured with Jensen's platinum-electrode at 2.5, 10, 20, and 50 cm depth from the soil surface weekly and more frequently after rains, and recorded with Jensen's ORP meter with reference electrode.

F.6 National Atmospheric Deposition Program (NADP)

- Purpose of network: nationwide network of stations for monitoring precipitation chemistry.
- Primary management agency: Multiple collaborative agencies. The program office is housed at the Illinois State Water Survey.
- Data website: http://nadp.sws.uiuc.edu.
- Measured weather/climate elements:
  - Precipitation.
  - Wet and dry deposition.
- Sampling frequency: daily for precipitation, weekly for other elements.
- Reporting frequency: weekly, but not accessible for many months.
- Estimated station cost: unknown.
- Network strengths:
  - Unique measurements.
  - High data standards.
- Network weaknesses:
  - Does not track most primary climate elements (e.g. temperature, wind).
  - Stations coverage is not dense and stations are spaced unevenly.
  - Sampling frequencies are only daily or weekly, depending on the element.

The NADP program is associated with the National Trends Network (NTN), the Mercury Deposition Network (MDN, 90 sites), and the Atmospheric Integrated Research Monitoring Network (AIRMoN, 9 sites). The NTN collects weekly precipitation samples that are analyzed for cations (hydrogen, calcium, sodium, magnesium, potassium, and ammonium) and anions (sulfate, nitrate, and chloride). The network began with 22 sites in 1978 and now counts 250 sites (2006) in the continental USA, Alaska, Puerto Rico and the Virgin Islands. This is a very large collaborative involving many federal, state, regional and local agencies, universities, non-governmental agencies, and private participants. Data are accessible via the web, but well after the fact (about 6 months).

F.7 National Data Buoy Center (NDBC)

- Purpose of network: moored buoys in near-shore to open-ocean environment to assist with maritime needs. These buoys are used for operations, weather analysis and diagnosis, and forecasting.
- Primary management agency: NDBC.
- Data website: http://www.ndbc.noaa.gov.
- Measured weather/climate elements:
  - Air temperature.
  - Water Temperature.
  - Relative humidity and/or dewpoint temperature.
  - Barometric Pressure.
  - Pressure tendency (3-hour change).
  - Wind speed, direction, gust.
  - Significant wave heights.
  - Wave periods.
  - Detailed wave summaries (chop, spectra, steepness, swell).

o Visibility.
o Ocean current speed and direction (some sites).
- Sampling frequency: every second.
- Reporting frequency: hourly.
- Estimated station cost: unknown.
- Network strengths:
  o Unique weather and climate data.
  o Data quality is excellent.
  o Site maintenance is excellent.
  o Site exposures are excellent.
  o Data are readily accessible.
  o Metadata are excellent.
  o Hourly data records are up to 20 years in length.
- Network weaknesses:
  o No precipitation (measurements would get contaminated by spray).

NDBC stations are large (3 m and 10 m diameter) rugged moored buoys off the coasts of North America in near shore to deep water conditions. These stations are generally quite reliable and are very durable. As of 2006 there were 98 data buoys deployed. Sites are quite important and are therefore given attention as needed.

F.8 Remote Automated Weather Station (RAWS)

- Purpose of network: provide near-real-time (hourly or near hourly) measurements of meteorological variables for use in fire weather forecasts and climatology. Data from RAWS also are used for natural resource management, flood forecasting, natural hazard management, and air-quality monitoring.
- Primary management agency: WRCC, National Interagency Fire Center.
- Data website: http://www.raws.dri.edu/index.html.
- Measured weather/climate elements:
  o Air temperature.
  o Precipitation.
  o Relative humidity.
  o Wind speed.
  o Wind direction.
  o Wind gust.
  o Gust direction.
  o Solar radiation.
  o Soil moisture and temperature.
- Sampling frequency: 1 or 10 minutes, element-dependent.
- Reporting frequency: generally hourly. Some stations report every 15 or 30 minutes.
- Estimated station cost: $12K with satellite telemetry ($8K without satellite telemetry); maintenance costs are around $2K/year.
- Network strengths:
  o Metadata records are usually complete.
  o Sites are located in remote areas.
  o Sites are generally well-maintained.

o Entire period of record available on-line.
- Network weaknesses:
  o RAWS network is focused largely on fire management needs (formerly focused only on fire needs).
  o Frozen precipitation is not measured reliably.
  o Station operation is not always continuous.
  o Data transmission is completed via one-way telemetry. Data are therefore recoverable either in real-time or not at all.

The RAWS network is used by many land-management agencies, such as the BLM, NPS, Fish and Wildlife Service, Bureau of Indian Affairs, Forest Service, and other agencies. The RAWS network was one of the first automated weather station networks to be installed in the United States. Most gauges do not have heaters, so hydrologic measurements are of little value when temperatures dip below freezing or reach freezing after frozen precipitation events. There are approximately 1,100 real-time sites in this network and about 1,800 historic sites (some are decommissioned or moved). The sites can transmit data all winter but may be in deep snow in some locations. The WRCC is the archive for this network and receives station data and metadata through a special connection to the National Interagency Fire Center in Boise, Idaho.

F.9 NWS Surface Airways Observation Program (SAO)

- Purpose of network: provide near-real-time (hourly or near hourly) measurements of meteorological variables and are used both for airport operations and weather forecasting.
- Primary management agency: NOAA, FAA.
- Data website: data are available from state climate offices, RCCs (e.g., WRCC, www.wrcc.dri.edu), and NCDC (www.ncdc.noaa.gov).
- Measured weather/climate elements:
  o Air temperature.
  o Dewpoint and/or relative humidity.
  o Wind speed.
  o Wind direction.
  o Wind gust.
  o Gust direction.
  o Barometric pressure.
  o Precipitation (not at many FAA sites).
  o Sky cover.
  o Ceiling (cloud height).
  o Visibility.
- Sampling frequency: element-dependent.
- Reporting frequency: element-dependent.
- Estimated station cost: $100–$200K with maintenance costs approximately $10K/year.
- Network strengths:
  o Records generally extend over several decades.
  o Consistent maintenance and station operations.
  o Data record is reasonably complete and usually high quality.
  o Hourly or sub-hourly data.
- Network weaknesses:

o Nearly all sites are located at airports.

o Data quality can be related to size of airport—smaller airports tend to have poorer datasets.

o Influences from urbanization and other land-use changes.

These stations are managed by NOAA, U. S. Navy, U. S. Air Force, and FAA. These stations are located generally at major airports and military bases. The FAA stations often do not record precipitation, or they may provide precipitation records of reduced quality. Automated stations are typically ASOSs for the NWS or AWOSs for the FAA. Some sites only report episodically with observers paid per observation.

F.10 USDA/NRCS Snowfall Telemetry (SNOTEL) network

- Purpose of network: collect snowpack and related climate data to assist in forecasting water supply in the western United States.
- Primary management agency: NRCS.
- Data website: http://www.wcc.nrcs.usda.gov/snow/.
- Measured weather/climate elements:
  o Air temperature.
  o Precipitation.
  o Snow water content.
  o Snow depth.
  o Relative humidity (enhanced sites only).
  o Wind speed (enhanced sites only).
  o Wind direction (enhanced sites only).
  o Solar radiation (enhanced sites only).
  o Soil moisture and temperature (enhanced sites only).
- Sampling frequency: 1-minute temperature; 1-hour precipitation, snow water content, and snow depth. Less than one minute for relative humidity, wind speed and direction, solar radiation, and soil moisture and temperature (all at enhanced site configurations only).
- Reporting frequency: reporting intervals are user-selectable. Commonly used intervals are every one, two, three, or six hours.
- Estimated station cost: $20K with maintenance costs approximately $2K/year.
- Network strengths:
  o Sites are located in high-altitude areas that typically do not have other weather or climate stations.
  o Data are of high quality and are largely complete.
  o Very reliable automated system.
- Network weaknesses:
  o Historically limited number of elements.
  o Remote so data gaps can be long.
  o Metadata sparse and not high quality; site histories are lacking.
  o Measurement and reporting frequencies vary.
  o Many hundreds of mountain ranges still not sampled.
  o Earliest stations were installed in the late 1970s; temperatures have only been recorded since the 1980s.

USDA/NRCS maintains a set of automated snow-monitoring stations known as the SNOTEL (snowfall telemetry) network. These stations are designed specifically for cold and snowy locations. Precipitation and snow water content measurements are intended for hydrologic applications and water-supply forecasting, so these measurements are measured generally to within 2.5 mm (0.1 in.). Snow depth is tracked to the nearest 25 mm (1 in.). These stations function year around.

F.11 USDA/NRCS Snowcourse Network (SC)

- Purpose of network: collect snowpack and related climate data to assist in forecasting water supply in the western United States.
- Primary management agency: NRCS.
- Data website: http://www.wcc.nrcs.usda.gov/snowcourse/.
- Measured weather/climate elements:
  o Snow depth.
  o Snow water equivalent.
- Measurement, reporting frequency: monthly or seasonally.
- Estimated station cost: cost of man-hours needed to set up snowcourse and make measurements.
- Network strengths
  o Periods of record are generally long.
  o Large number of high-altitude sites.
- Network weaknesses
  o Measurement and reporting only occurs on monthly to seasonal basis.
  o Few weather/climate elements are measured.

USDA/NRCS maintains another network of snow-monitoring stations in addition to SNOTEL. These sites are known as snowcourses. Many of these sites have been in operation since the early part of the twentieth century. These are all manual sites where only snow depth and snow water content are measured.

F.12 USDA/NRCS Aerial Markers (NRCS-AM)

- Purpose of network: supplement snow data for water supply forecasts in Alaska.
- Primary management agency: NRCS.
- Data website: http://www.wcc.nrcs.usda.gov/snowcourse/.
- Measured weather/climate elements:
  o Snow depth.
- Sampling frequency: monthly or seasonally, spring only.
- Reporting frequency: monthly or seasonally, spring only.
- Estimated station cost: cost of a steel pole with depth markers visible from an airplane, with marker sign on top.
- Network strengths:
  o Earliest records start in 1920s and 1930s; many records are 50-60 years long.
  o Many sites are high-altitude sites.
  o Site maintenance is excellent.
- Network weaknesses:
  o Sampling and reporting frequencies.

o Only measures snow depth.

o Few sites currently in operation.

The NRCS-AM sites were a supplement to the snow courses, which were the precursor to the SNOTEL network. A plane typically visits a given site near the end of the month and notes the snow depth as indicated on a calibrated steel pole with large markers that are visible from a distance. No other information is recorded other than snow depth.

F.13 Radiosonde/Rawinsonde stations (Upper Air)

- Purpose of network: provide upper air measurements as part of the global observing system.
- Primary management agency: NOAA and national governments.
- Data website: http://www.nws.noaa.gov/ops2/ua/.
- Measured weather/climate elements:
  o Air temperature.
  o Barometric pressure.
  o Relative humidity.
  o Wind speed and direction.
- Sampling frequency: deployments are twice daily, at 0000 and 1200 GMT; for each deployment, sampling occurs every 6 seconds.
- Reporting frequency: twice daily, at 0000 and 1200 GMT; for each deployment, reporting occurs every 6 seconds.
- Estimated station cost: the suite of sensors on each deployment costs about $100. About half of the sensors are recovered from each deployment, to be refurbished for use in other deployments.
- Network strengths:
  o Excellent data quality.
  o High spatial resolution.
  o Provides only available long-term measurements of free atmosphere. Records are up to 60 years for some sites.
  o Very important for weather forecasting, so there are few data gaps.
- Network weaknesses:
  o Only twice-daily measurements.
  o Sites are far apart (100-200 km).
  o Some sites have moved occasionally.

The upper air network is a benchmark dataset that extends from just after World War II, and earlier in a few locations. There are about 70 sites in the contiguous USA, another 12 in Alaska, and 9 in the Pacific Islands, and a total of 92 over North America. The hydrogen filled balloons rise until they burst (usually at about 30-32 km altitude), and then instruments float back to earth via parachute, where they can be refurbished if recovered. Most sites have at least 20-30 years of records. Some changes made to network in mid 1990s. These are our only reliable source of detailed systematic vertical information about the atmosphere. Measurements are made at mandatory pressure levels, including the surface, 925 mb (800 m above sea level), 850 mb (1600 m), 700 mb (3,000 m) and 500 mb (5,000 m). WRCC stores the historical and real-time data for these sites.

Appendix G. Selected Alaska climate maps.

Maps are based on PRISM data from 1961-1990.

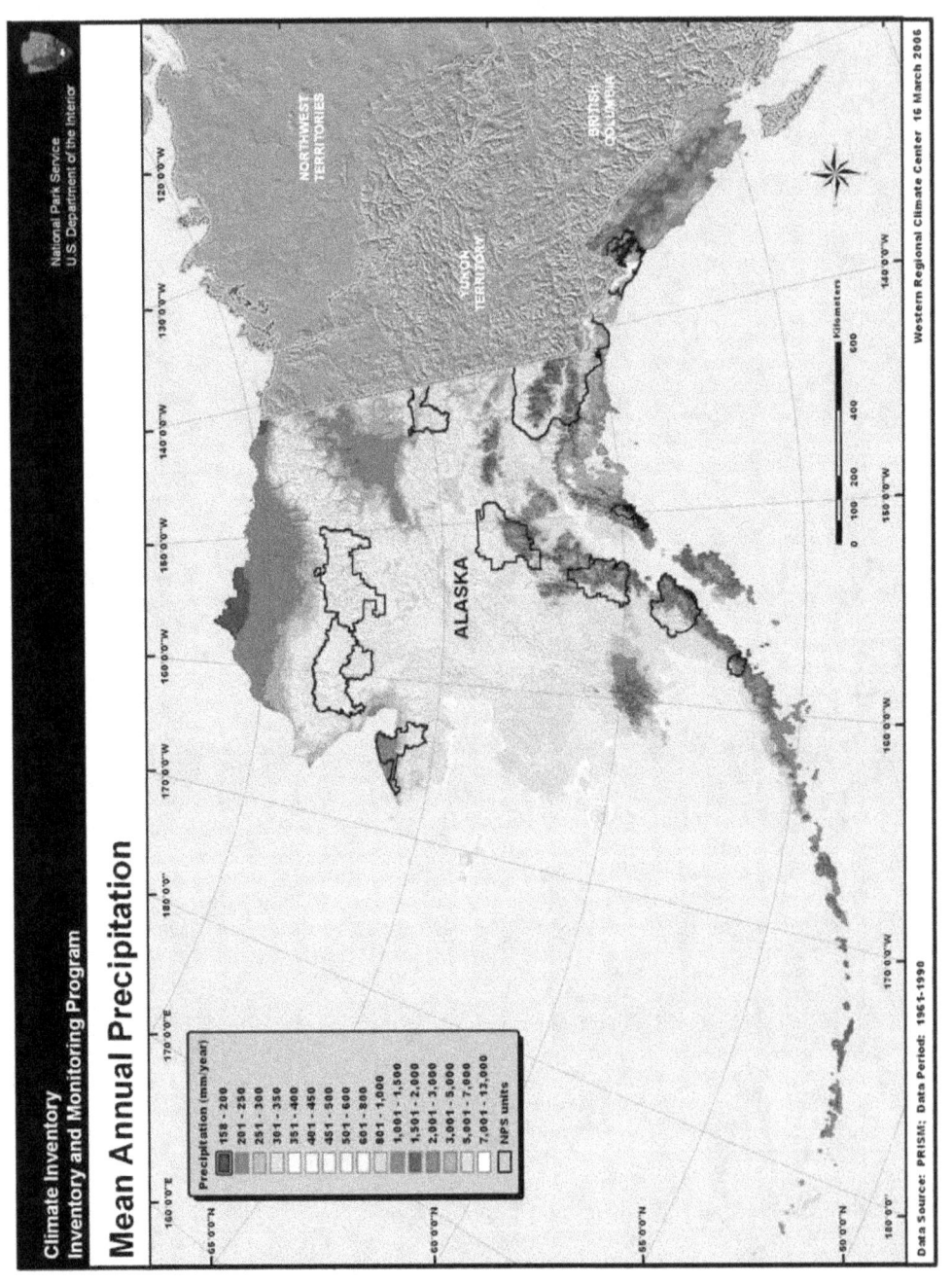

Figure G.1. Mean annual precipitation for Alaska, 1961-1990.

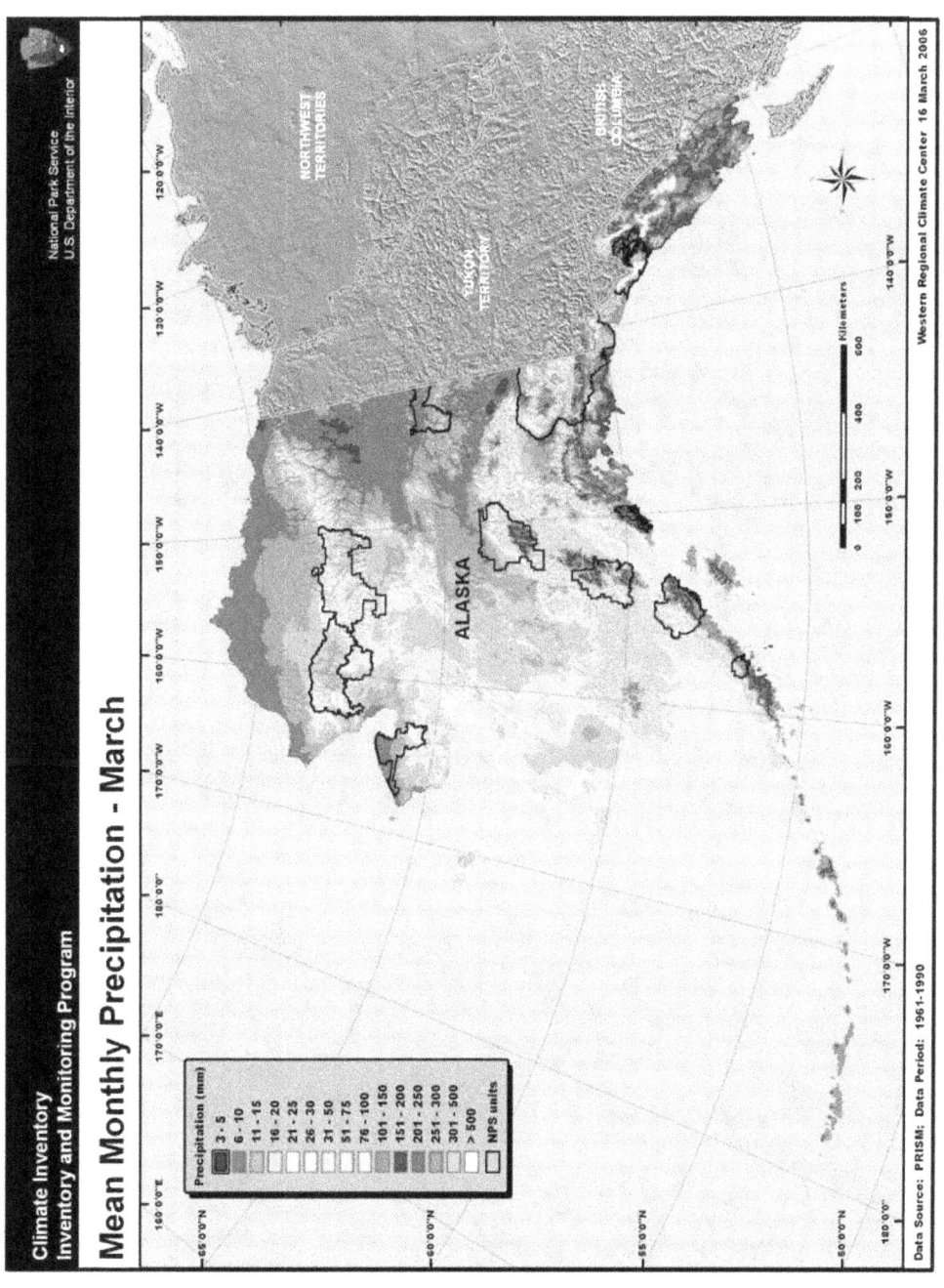

Figure G.2. Mean March precipitation for Alaska, 1961-1990.

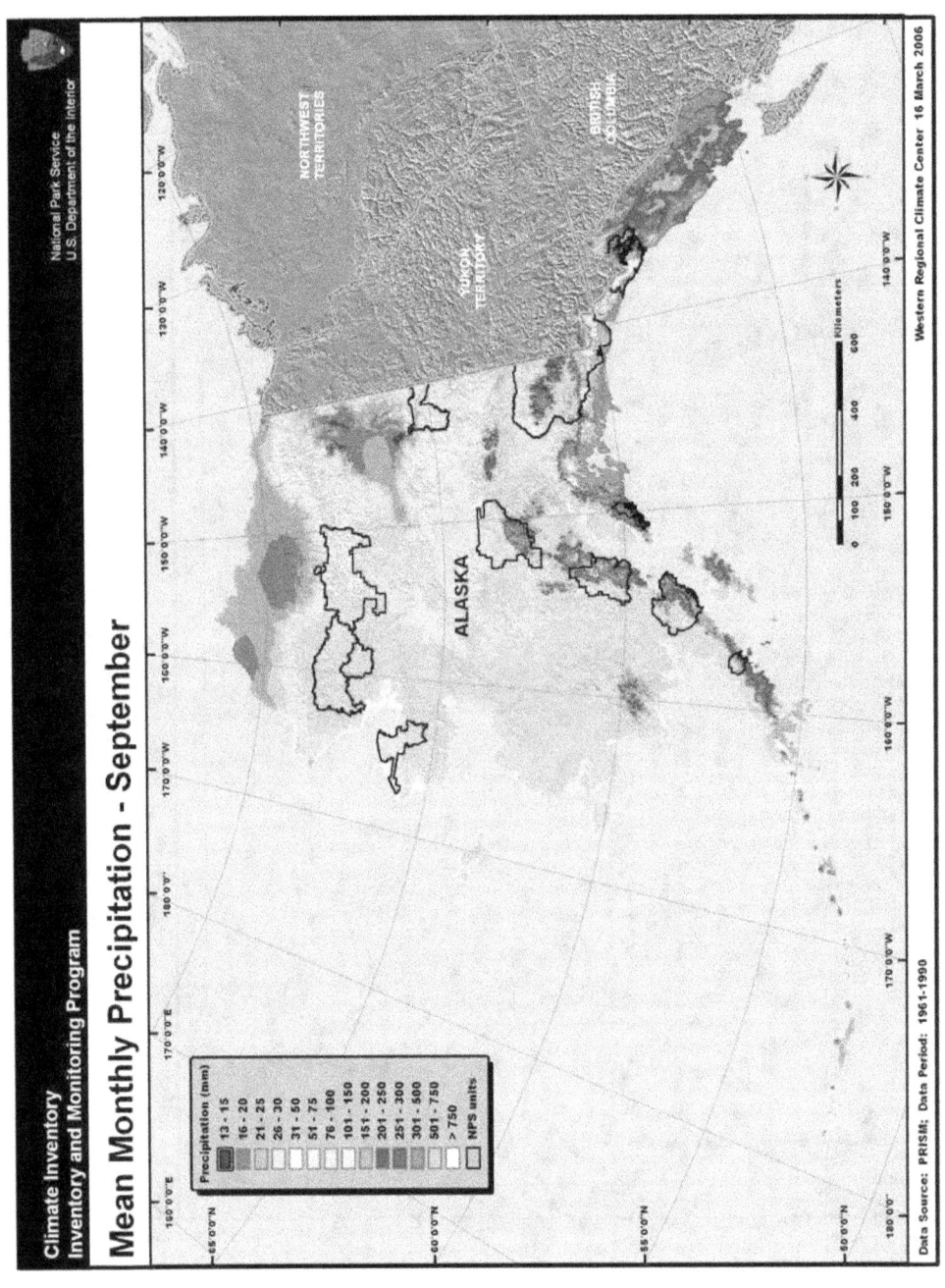

Figure G.3. Mean September precipitation for Alaska, 1961-1990.

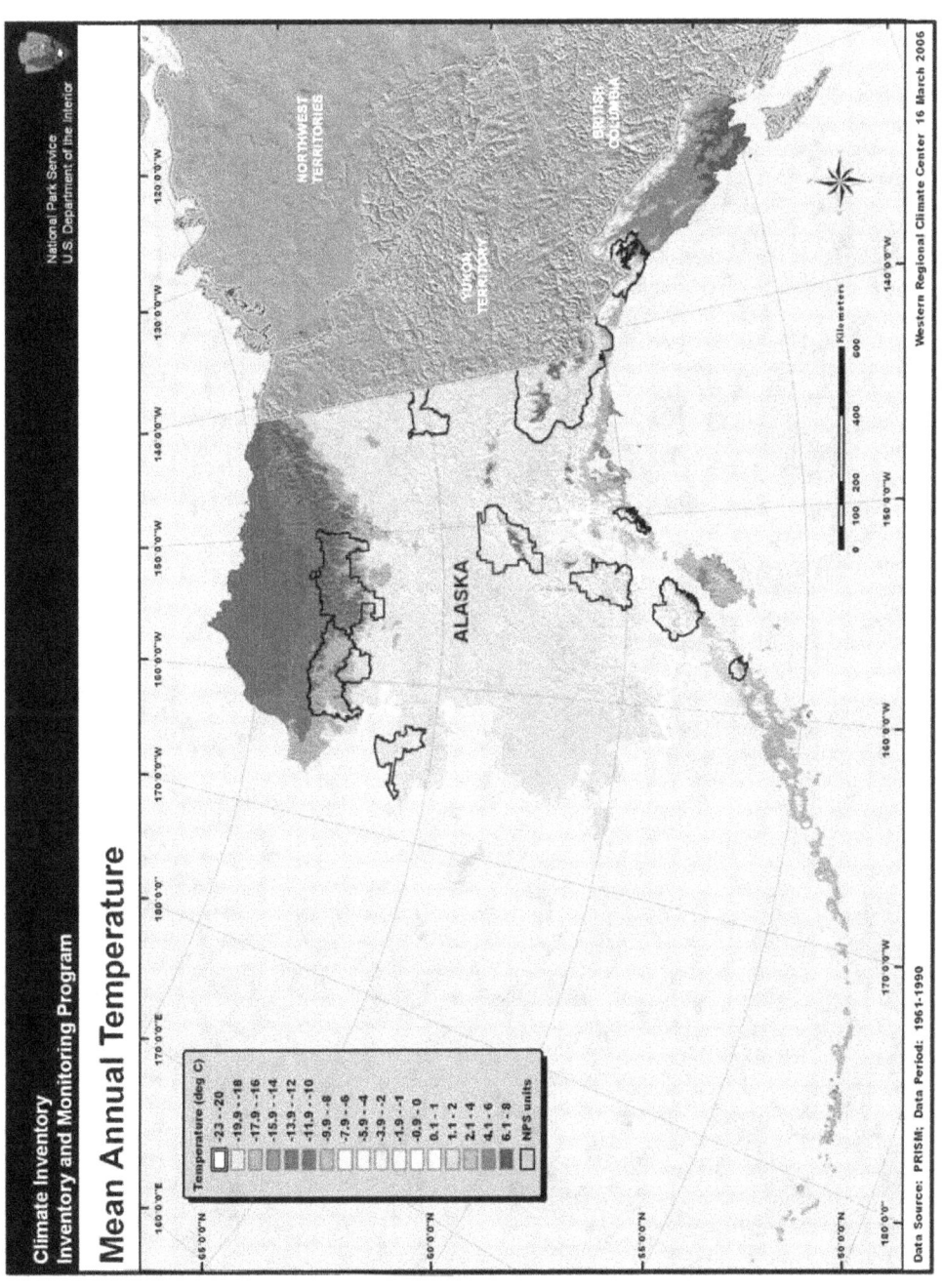

Figure G.4. Mean annual temperature for Alaska, 1961-1990.

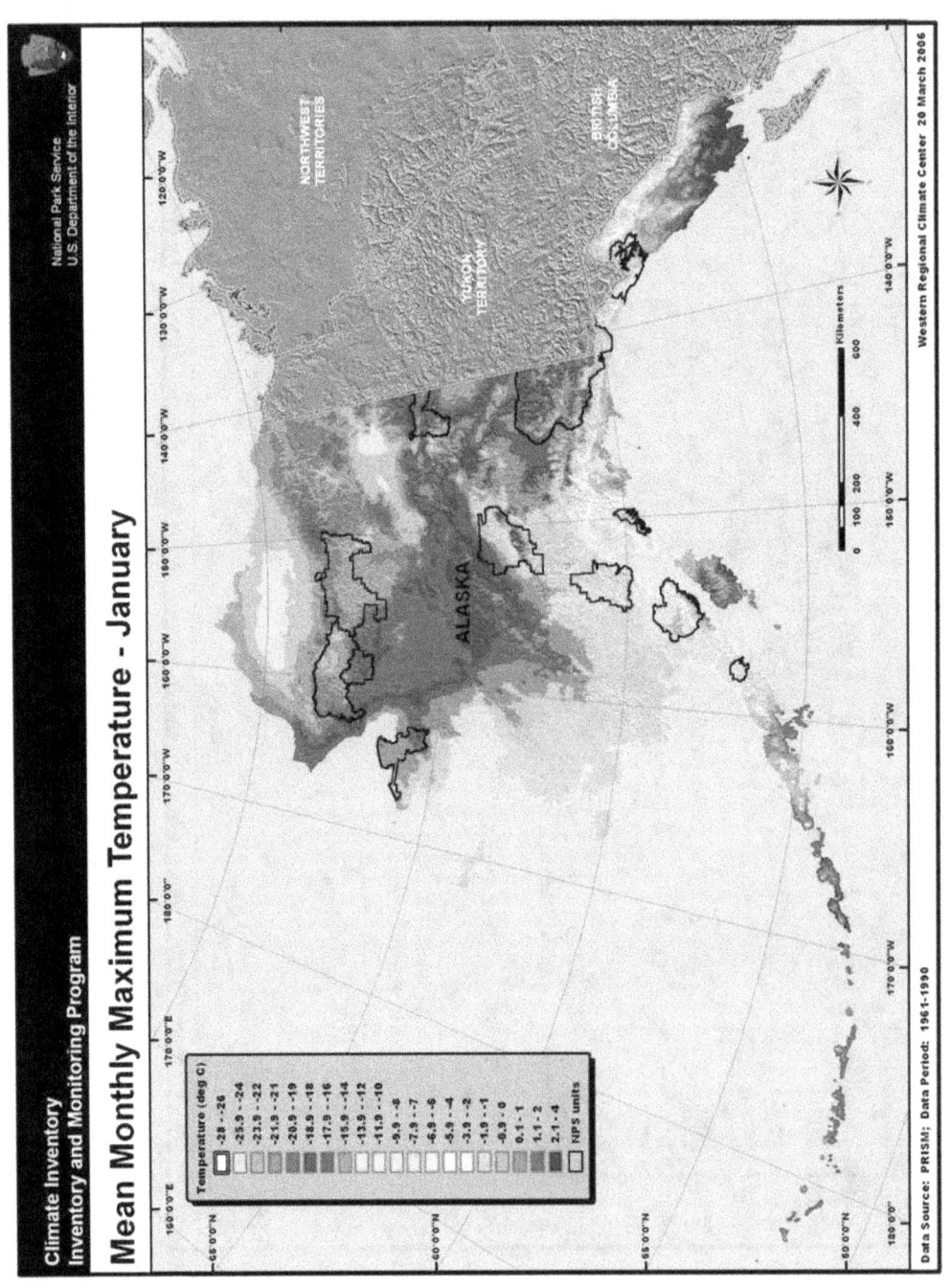

Figure G.5. Mean January maximum temperature for Alaska, 1961-1990.

104

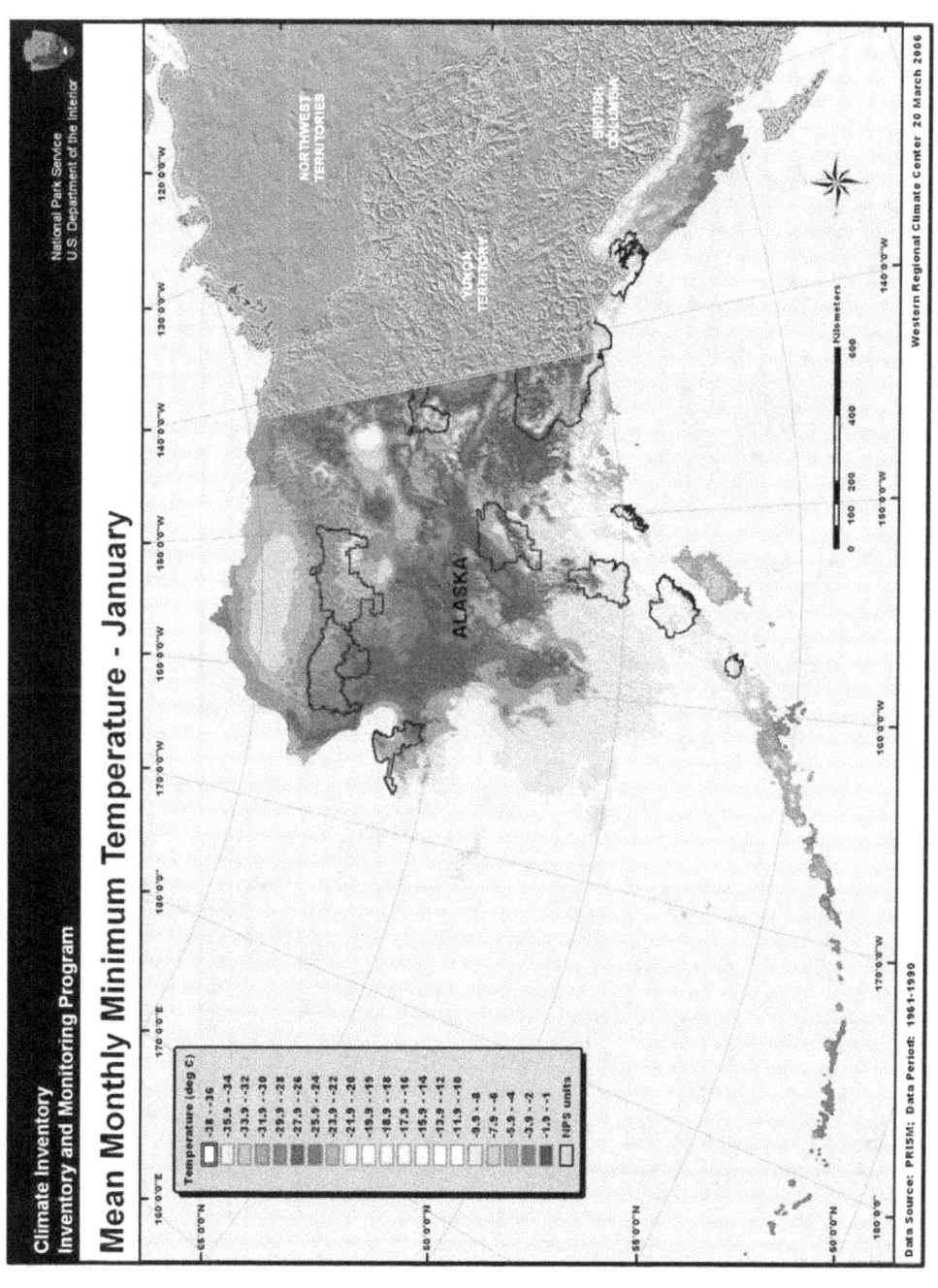

Figure G.6.   Mean January minimum temperature for Alaska, 1961-1990.

105

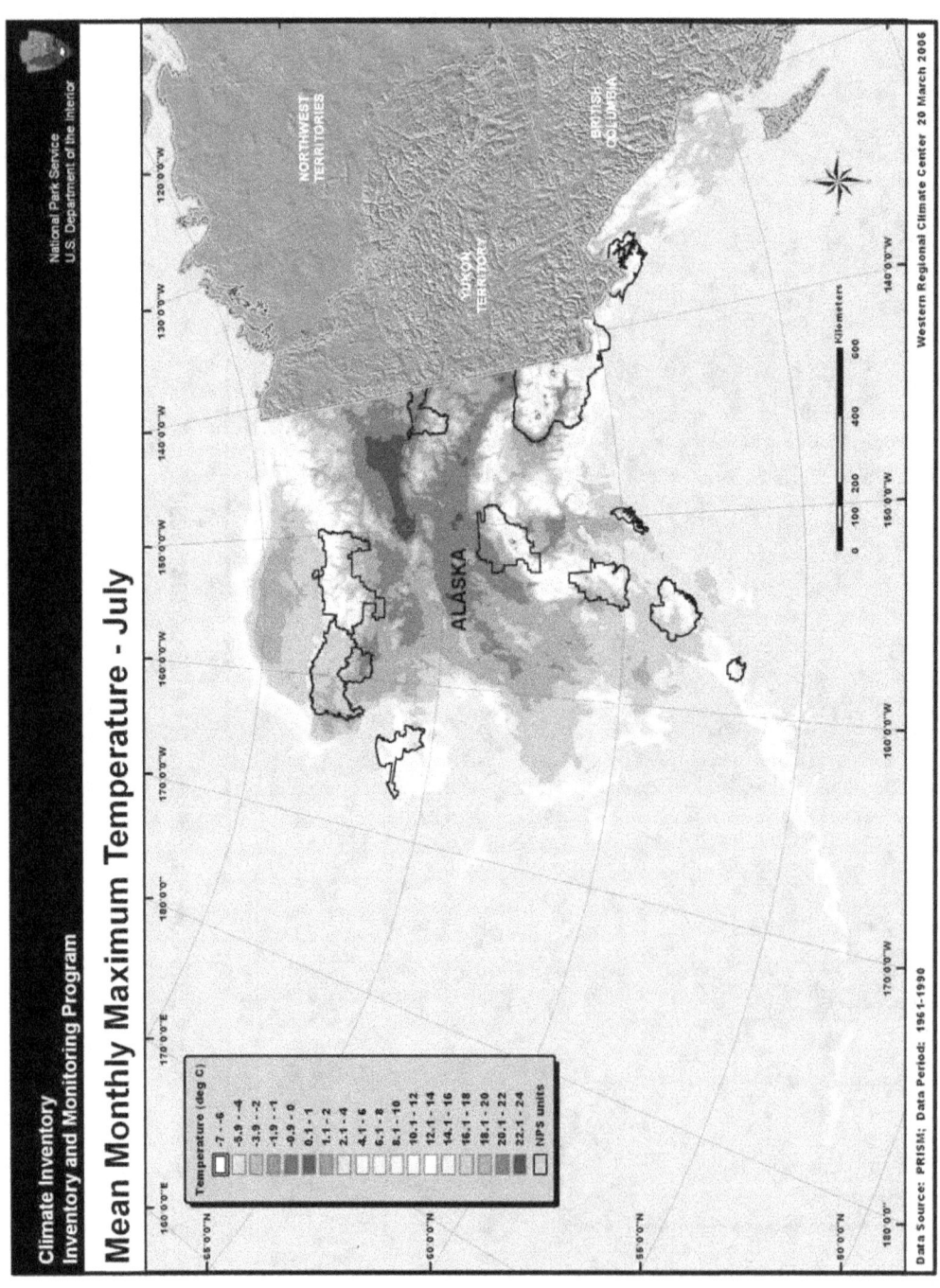

Figure G.7. Mean July maximum temperature for Alaska, 1961-1990.

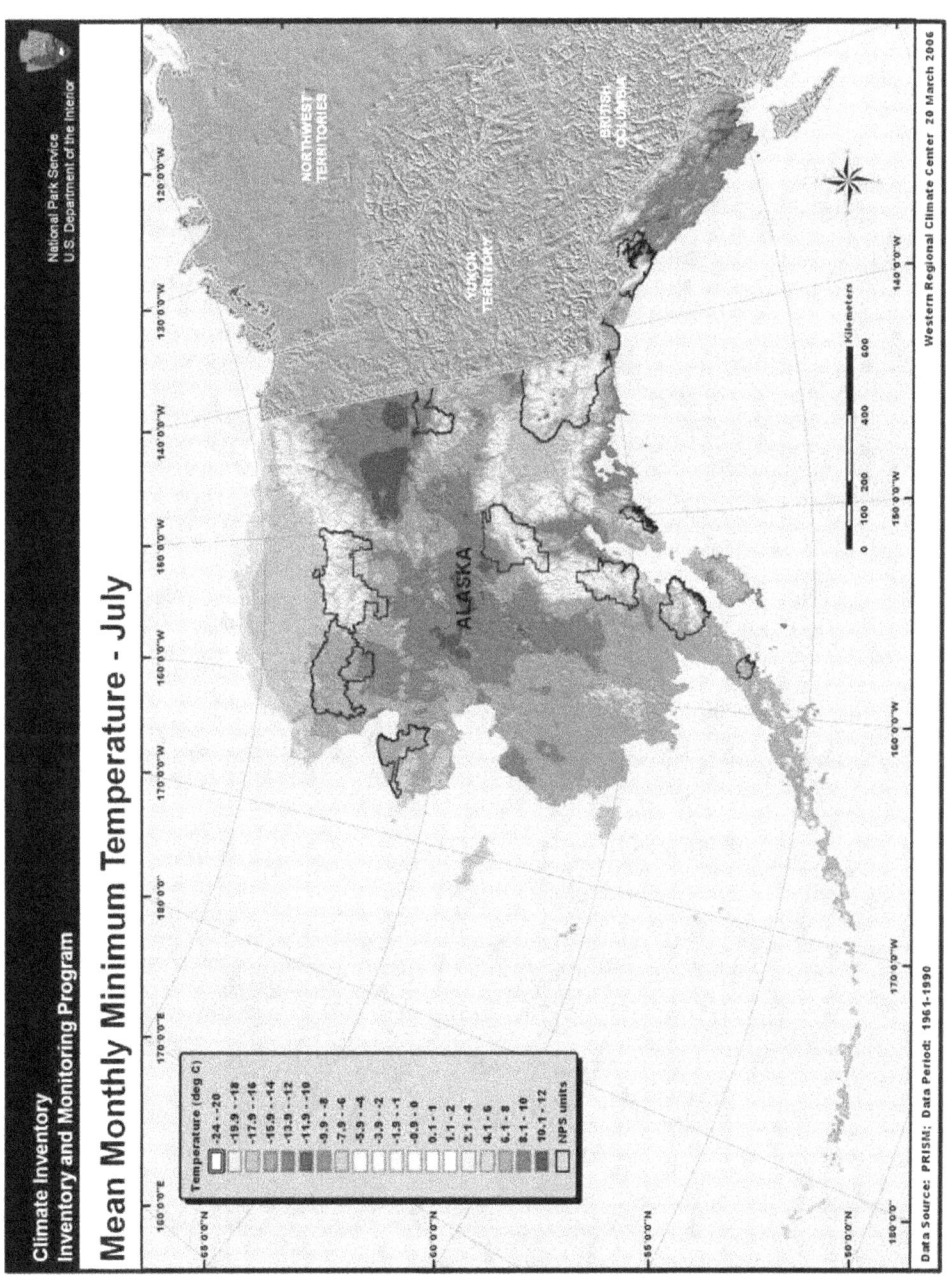

Figure G.8. Mean July minimum temperature for Alaska, 1961-1990.

107

Appendix H. Electronic supplements.

H.1 ACIS metadata file for weather and climate stations associated with the CAKN:
http://www.wrcc.dri.edu/nps/pub/cakn/reports/CAKN_from_ACIS.tar.gz.

H.2 CAKN metadata files for weather and climate stations associated with the CAKN:
http://www.wrcc.dri.edu/nps/pub/cakn/metadata/CAKN_cli_sta.tar.gz.

NPS/CAKN/NRTR—2006/004, August 2006